Using Technology to Transform the Value Chain

Using Technology to Transform the Value Chain

Fred Kuglin • Ray Hood

CRC Press
Taylor & Francis Group
Boca Raton   London   New York

CRC Press is an imprint of the
Taylor & Francis Group, an **informa** business

Auerbach Publications
Taylor & Francis Group
6000 Broken Sound Parkway NW, Suite 300
Boca Raton, FL 33487-2742

International Standard Book Number-13: 978-1-4200-4759-2 (Hardcover)

Library of Congress Cataloging-in-Publication Data

Kuglin, Fred A.
    Using technology to transform the value chain / Fred Kuglin, Ray Hood.
        p. cm.
    Includes bibliographical references and index.
    ISBN 978-1-4200-4759-2 (alk. paper)
    1. Business logistics. I. Hood, Ray V. II. Title.

HD38.5.K849 2008
658.5'14--dc22   2008044082

Visit the Taylor & Francis Web site at
http://www.taylorandfrancis.com

and the Auerbach Web site at
http://www.auerbach-publications.com

Contents

Acknowledgments

The inspiration for us to write this book came from multiple personal and professional sources. The growing impact of applying new technologies in the global value chain never ceases to amaze us. Our level of amazement is only exceeded by the pace of change in technology overall. The next decade will be one of increasing opportunity for professionals on the leading edge of applying technology—and one of increasing peril for those who choose to be laggards.

Fred: A special thank you goes to my wife Karin and children Heidi and Karl for their support, understanding, and occasional assistance throughout the writing process. In addition, I want to thank Dr. Les Waters for his ongoing mentoring and support. Also, I want to thank my co-author, Ray Hood, for his significant contributions. It was a pleasure to work with Ray, who is a brilliant business executive, a wonderful family man, and a friend.

Ray: To my wife Stefani, who puts up with my long hours, I owe a great debt of gratitude. To my three sons, Tripp, Reid, and Jack, your world will be so different from mine. The changes over the next 50 years will make the last 50 look like a warm-up.

To Fred Kuglin, who was the driving force behind this effort, thank you for keeping me on track. One of these days, I will think of a way to show him proper thanks.

Joint: We want to thank the following individuals for their specific contributions to individual chapters: Scot Stelter of Alien Technology, Karen Jensen of Printronix, and Sherita Coffeit of N.T.T.A for Chapter 1; Sherry Farley of CADEC, Kliff Black of SensorLogic, and Peter Maysek of SensiTech for Chapter 2; Randy Krueger of Cargill, Dr. Ramon Bonfil, Patrich Simpkins of SensorLogic, and William Buckley of GPS Tracking System.net for Chapter 3; Theresa Arosemena of the Panama Canal Authority, Heather Lepeska and Kendall Shiffler of the Inland International Port of Dallas/City of Dallas, the Union Pacific Railroad, and Paul and Kathy Orsak of ZMS Technologies for Chapter 5; Harold Anderson, CLS, an Inmar Company of Carolina Logistics, Marc Daigle and Craig Stamm of Authentix for Chapter 7; and Brendan Ziolo and Krishna Kurapati of Sipera Systems for Chapter 8. Finally, all quotations not specifically referenced in the endnotes come from our personal interviews and experiences.

Introduction

Overview

An efficient and effective supply chain manages the flow of goods, the flow of information, and the generation and reporting of related financial transactions. The flow of goods involves the managing of customer orders through a network of suppliers and distribution centers to a customer delivery point. The flow of information involves the data collection supporting the flow of goods, the conversion of these data to useful information, and the sharing of this information across the multiple supply chain partners to enhance the supply chain's performance in managing the flow of goods. As goods pass from one supply chain partner to another, financial transactions are created. These financial transactions convert the goods into cash, creating a series of reports on cash flows and performance measurements.

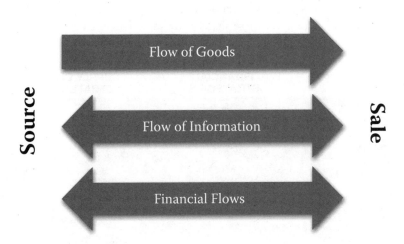

The complexity increases as organizational priorities unfold. The CEO and his or her direct reports have a tight correlation to the agenda of the board of directors. This agenda changes throughout the year, and is usually focused on mergers, acquisitions, and all other activities (e.g., increasing sales, decreasing costs, leveraging fixed assets, accelerating working capital turns, and minimizing effective tax rates) that drive shareholder value. The profit and loss (P&L) owners (senior vice presidents and vice presidents) are focused on the execution of their annual operating plan. This annual operating plan, frequently completed in the fourth quarter of the previous fiscal year, dictates performance targets on increasing revenues, decreasing costs, and available capital to invest. The operating expense budget owners (directors, managers) are focused on execution tasks and managing to their direct costs. As the board agenda changes due to internal and external forces, it becomes increasingly difficult to coordinate or connect the activities of the P&L owners and operating expense budget owners to ensure alignment with the current board agenda. (Does anyone ever feel that his or her organization is a little disjointed at times?)

Throughout the chapters in the book, we try to "connect the several dots" that represent the complex world of supply chain management. We provide specific reviews of the execution activities of moving goods; specific reviews of existing and new technologies that enable the flow of information; specific reviews of technology architectures that pull together the hardware, software, and middleware necessary for the effective flow of information; and specific reviews of industry supply chains. In most cases, we incorporate the financial performance metrics that govern the financial transactions and their associated value propositions. The effective use of information not only reduces costs, but also helps increase sales through connectivity to customers and markets, enables greater use of fixed assets, helps accelerate working capital turns, and enables acquisitions. The information throughout the supply chain is at the heart of all of these shareholder value measurements. Maximizing shareholder value requires supply chain excellence in most companies.

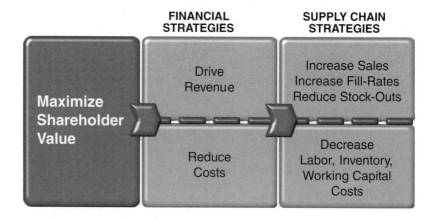

Where Are We Today?

Overall, the consensus among industry executives is that global supply chain executives have performed very well in managing the flow of goods in the past several years. However, there is a strong feeling among these same executives that the application of technology within the supply chain to manage the flow of information has not kept pace with available technologies and the need for these technologies. These executives feel that the lack of the flow of quality information has hindered their supply chains' performances.

If the flow of information is so important to the flow of goods and the flow of money from the financial transactions, then how did we get to this point? To help understand where we are today, we will look at immediate history to help understand the "why we are here."

The Era of "Technology Fatigue"

During the 1990s, there was a huge technology boom in the global economy. Fueled by years of dis-investment, technological advances, and the fear (justified and unjustified) of the "Y2K" issue, companies invested massive amounts of capital into their technology infrastructures. It was literally a golden era for the enterprise resource planning and the supply chain software industries.

From November 1999 through the end of 2001, three events occurred that affected the overall investment level in technology. January 1, 2000 came and went, causing some disruption but effectively ending the Y2K spending in technology.

Effect of the Dot Com/Y2K Bubble and Crash on IT Spending

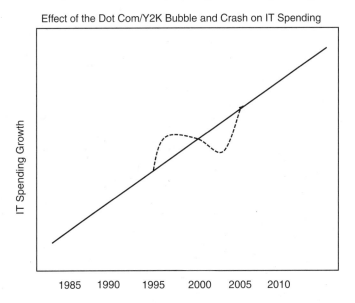

The "tech bubble" burst in 2000, and the terrorist attacks of September 11, 2001 caused disruption in consumer confidence and contributed to a mild recession.

As is typical with boards of directors and their moving agendas, the pendulum swung the other way. In the 1990s, enterprise resource planning (ERP) implementations and major supply chain software purchases approaching $100+ million were frequently approved overnight and without business cases. One major ERP company tracked all sales over $50 million. For the last half of the 1990s, almost 50 percent of this ERP company's $50+ million sales were approved by their customers without formal business cases justifying the expenditures! One major supply chain software company frequently employed the fear tactic of selling to their customers' prime competitors to get quick approval on $10 to $50 million software projects. Supply chain professionals often approved the purchase of supply chain software with no cost/benefit analysis, yet received promotions for their quick action. By the end of 2001, boards of directors were asking, "What did I get for my investments in technology?" Most of the time, the answer was: "Some benefit, but no where near the level needed to justify the level of expenditures." The era of "technology fatigue" had begun.

Living with the Outcomes of Over-Reacting

By the start of 2002, many companies realigned their organizations to have their chief information officer (CIO) and their senior supply chain executives report to the chief financial officer (CFO). Both information technology (IT) and supply chain professionals found themselves operating with a new set of organizational realities. The CFOs were driven by lower supply chain execution costs and harnessing the "out-of-control" IT expenditures. The unrelenting cost-focus of the CFOs discouraged capital investments and caused a dramatic curtailment of their IT spending.

This pendulum swing toward total cost control and away from technology investments was very unfortunate from a timing perspective. Since the end of the tech bubble and 9/11, there has been a dramatic increase in breakthrough technologies supporting supply chain management. These technologies affect the supply chain both directly (technologies involving sensors and wireless) and indirectly (technologies creating the new DVD format and the digital supply chain). When combining these new technologies with the significant shift in the global economies since 2001, the result is a new operating environment for global supply chain (and global business) leaders. In many respects, these leaders were not prepared for this dramatic of shift in such a short period. Their response? Follow the leader and look for the "silver bullet."

The Leader = Wal-Mart! The Silver Bullet = RFID?

At the time of this pendulum swing to total cost control, Wal-Mart and the U.S. Department of Defense (DoD) were initiating their radio frequency identification

(RFID) programs. Wal-Mart's program, designed to enable Wal-Mart to increase the throughput of their supply chain by approximately 50 percent without any increase in capital investment, was theoretically logical but way ahead of its time from a technology maturation standpoint. Discouraged to pursue new technologies, reporting to CFOs, and with RFID dominating the industry headlines thanks to Wal-Mart (and the DoD), supply chain professionals took the easy road and automatically defaulted to their industry positions on RFID when considering new technologies. By default and ahead of its maturation, RFID emerged as "the new supply chain technology" to most supply chain professionals.

During the timeframe since 2001, many industries have explored the use of RFID technology in their supply chains as the result of mandates by Wal-Mart and the DoD to establish their industry positions. In addition, companies invested time, money, and resources in RFID pilot and compliance programs mandated by Wal-Mart and the DoD. Becausee most of these pilot programs produced minimal benefits versus their investment levels, it was politically correct for supply chain professionals only to do the minimum required by Wal-Mart and the DoD to keep them as customers.

All these trends are very unfortunate for three reasons. First, as we mentioned, the RFID technology has many significant maturation issues that may take up to ten years to address. Second, other technologies have emerged to offer solid returns on their investments, but have been overlooked by the default attention to RFID. Third, technologies have emerged that have transformed products and entire supply chains without RFID being involved. We will cover all three points throughout the chapters in the book.

Technology and the Structural Changes of Supply Chains

If the recent trends since 2001 were not enough, technologies have emerged to drive structural changes in global supply chains. Some of these structural changes have proven to be challenging for even the most seasoned supply chain professionals. The "digital" supply chain in the media industry is rapidly growing due to emerging technologies and must be concurrently managed with the "physical" supply chain. The world of ocean container shipping is large, complex, slow-to-change, and misunderstood by many supply chain practitioners. This segment of the global supply chain is usually "outsourced" to third parties as a way to deal with its complexities. The traditional slow-moving, repetitive nature of this industry is a natural fit for third-party logistics (3pls) companies. However, emerging technologies (with macro-economic forces) are driving changes even in this stoic, slow-moving industry segment, in many cases moving the industry beyond the normal capabilities of 3pls. Supply chain professionals must reintroduce themselves to this industry segment due to its cost impact on their companies.

Our Focus in This Book

There may be a silver lining emerging with supply chain executives and CIOs reporting to CFOs. The CFOs may be "seeing the light." IBM, in its IBM 2005 Global CFO Study, reported that finance organizations plan to redouble efforts involving process ownership and process mapping. Underlying the process ownership is a major shift away from viewing data and information as the property and responsibility of its business units and toward the view that data and information are corporate assets that should be leveraged throughout the extended supply chain.*

In this book, we will address the use of data and information as a corporate asset to be leveraged throughout the supply chain. We will review "the default supply chain technology" RFID and the new technologies affecting supply chain professionals. We will address these issues as they affect specific industry segments in each chapter. Throughout the book, special emphasis will be placed on the cost/benefit metrics supporting the application and use of these technologies throughout the supply chain processes.

It is important for us to note that technology alone does nothing for global companies. When applied to business processes in an effective way, new technologies can produce breakthrough changes in how companies do business. Many global industries suffer from over-capacity and fierce competition for their products and services. In addition, many product-based companies are realizing that value-added services after the product sale can produce streams of revenues that are a multiple of the original products' revenues. These value-added services rely heavily on newer technologies, especially those using advanced sensors and wireless technology to detect imminent problems and resolve them through communications to the right party.

Despite the results from the IBM study, we observe that several industry executives are waiting—waiting for the maturation of RFID, waiting for the U.S. government to mandate the use of new technologies, or waiting for the "lead elephant" in their industry sector to be an early adopter of new technologies. Unfortunately, waiting will have serious consequences for many companies. Counterfeit drugs are increasingly becoming a danger to consumers; pork producers are watching their farmers decrease in number due to ageing and retirement; movie studios are watching their content being downloaded on the Internet in record numbers; and global shippers are watching the delay time through the major U.S. ports go through the roof, significantly disrupting order-to-delivery times. These consequences have measurable cost impacts to their companies, placing a huge penalty on those who wait. Our book is designed to help the supply chain professional find new ways and technologies to modify their supply chain processes within the cost/benefit boundaries of their CFOs—and stop the waiting!

---

* http://www-935.ibm.com/services/us/gbs/bus/html/2005_cfo_survey_gen.html, Survey Results.

The Book—Chapter by Chapter

Chapter 1: Radio Frequency Identification: Cure for Cancer or Supplier Curse?

Our journey in this book begins with an in-depth review of RFID technology. In Chapter 1, we discuss the Wal-Mart initiative and trace the first uses of RFID technology back to the early days of World War II. We state that, using "hype" and "time," there are five stages of emerging technology: technology trigger, peak of inflated expectations, trough of disillusionment, slope of enlightenment, and plateau of productivity. With the current state of the maturation of RFID technology, we believe that this technology is in the trough of disillusionment stage and will begin to enter the slope of enlightenment stage in the next few years.

In Chapter 1, we proceed to discuss the components of an RFID solution. We delve into RFID tags, and discuss the differences between passive, semi-active, and active tags. We follow our discussions with a review of RFID readers and the four frequencies used for RFID technology; these frequencies are "low" (~125 kHz), "high" (13.56 MHz), "ultra-high" or UHF (902 to 928 MHz), and microwave (2.45 GHZ). More importantly, we discuss the lack of an agreed-to global frequency for use by global supply chain participants and how this lack of a common frequency inhibits the effective (and potential) use of RFID for global shipments.

We proceed to discuss the potential application of RFID technology in a supply chain. We cite the issues of reader collision and the modification of readers to accommodate or work around these collisions by putting the readers "to sleep" at selected times. In addition, we discuss in depth the issue of misreads and the economics around these misreads. We proceed to review the costs and benefits of current RFID implementations, and cite specific reasons for the supplier resistance in the marketplace today.

Toward the end of Chapter 1, we discuss three automotive applications of RFID technology and review the success and shortcomings of its implementation in the three applications. We proceed to identify specific applications (transit systems, toll roads, and human implants) where RFID technology implementations are considered solid successes. We summarize the chapter with a review of the limited success Wal-Mart has experienced with RFID (reducing stock-outs, better warehouse management processes that contribute to higher order-fill rates) and the lack of success experienced by its suppliers. We conclude that the future of RFID technology continues to hold promise, with the technology emerging out of the trough of disillusionment in the next few years with more maturation.

Chapter 2: Wireless Sensors: The Value-Based World beyond Radio Frequency Identification

Our journey continues in Chapter 2 with the introduction of sensors as a complimentary supply chain technology to RFID. We discuss the definition of a sensor and review the modern history of sensors dating back to the late 1800s. In Chapter 2, we review the dual role of sensors in supply chains, with fixed assets being one role and mobile assets being the other.

We review sensors, RFID, and barcodes, using a food industry example to highlight their commonalities and differences. The value proposition of using sensors on fixed assets is introduced, using the automotive industry, food industry, and other examples. We progress to the value proposition involving the use of sensors to monitor the moving asset. In this area, we display Cadec systems and the evolution of its technologies in monitoring and interacting with moving assets. We bridge our overview of Cadec to an in-depth review of wireless local area networks (WLANs). This includes a review of how Cadec uses Wi-Fi centers to connect to its designated WLANs.

We transition from monitoring and interacting with the moving assets to monitoring the conditions inside the transport trailers. Sensitech, a division of Carrier Corporation, is introduced as a company that excels in the diagnostics of what happens to the cargo as conditions inside a transport trailer change during the transport trip.

The need to interact with the transportation asset to manage the conditions within a trailer to protect the cargo in a near real-time manner is introduced. We discuss the costs and benefits of using satellite communications, and introduce the use of cellular technology as an alternative to satellite technology. The different technologies in use in cellular communications are defined (GSM, GPRS, and CDMA 2000) to help the supply chain professional distinguish between their costs, complexities, and benefits.

Toward the end of Chapter 2, we discuss an in-depth "success story" involving a leading transportation insurance company. This success story traces their actual experiences with sensors from a security standpoint, and how the use of sensors advanced as the "bad guys" learned how to bypass the sensors at different stages of development. At the end of Chapter 2, we conclude that the use of sensors provides a powerful complement to the use of RFID technology in the supply chain, and helps the supply chain professional take their performance to the next level.

Chapter 3: Tracking Animals and Other Living Beings: From Farm to Fork and from Home to School (Hopefully!)

Building on Chapter 1 (RFID) and Chapter 2 (sensors), we focus in Chapter 3 on the use of both technologies to track animals, specifically hogs from "farm to fork." We extend this focus to include the tracking of marine life, pets, and people.

Our review of the pork supply chain begins with an overview of the size of the global pork industry and the importance of this industry to selected countries. We proceed with our supply chain analysis from the start of the pork supply chain, the birth process. We follow this analysis with a discussion on the roles of the "integrators" and the "growers" in getting the piglets from nurseries to hogs in finishing houses. A review of the optimal processing weight closes out the "wean to finish" process.

An analysis of the "pro forma hog P&L" identifies the largest cost categories as the feeder pigs themselves, the feed for the pigs, and the capital costs to outfit the farrowing facilities and grow houses. An in-depth look at SensorLogic's "Smart-Farm" solution to control the environment in the barns allowed us to connect the use of sensors and wireless communications to controlling the environment within the barns and, as a result, the feed and infrastructure costs of the hog P&L.

The processing plant to store-shelf portion of the pork supply chain identifies how sensors with RFID technology tracked the "batches" of hogs from the processing plant through the tray packing plants to the store shelves. The replenishment of the store shelves and the influence (or lack thereof) on the store door price of pork products is reviewed, along with category management. This provides a discussion on the costs of supply disruptions to both suppliers and retailers.

We review the tracking of marine life, with a look at Sonotronics and their marine life tracking solution. In addition, we review tracking livestock with a focus on TekVet and its Teksensor, an active RFID tag placed on the cow's ear. In both cases, we show how the tracking of marine life and cattle contributes to the knowledge of their environment and ultimately their health. We return to the future of tracking hogs through the pork supply chain and its importance to control diseases.

We cover the tracking of pets toward the end of the chapter. Emphasis is placed on the size of the problem of lost pets. We also review Micro Tech's GPS Pet Tracker X5000, GPS Tracking Systems' globalpetfinder, and Pointer Positioning Solutions's radar system as working pet tracking solutions in 2008. We conclude the chapter with a notation on the tracking of people (from criminals to the memory impaired).

Chapter 4: The Media Supply Chain Key Word: Digital

In Chapter 4, we shift our focus from the physical to the digital supply chain. We begin the chapter by examining the size of the media and entertainment industry. We progress by reviewing the history of the Betamax versus VHS battle between Sony and Toshiba in the 1980s. This review leads us into the battle in 2008 for the next generation DVD format between the Sony-led Blu-ray Disc Association and the Toshiba-led HD DVD group. We discuss the winners (perceived and real) from the battle in the 1980s and the implications of the current battle to the supply chain professionals.

We next discuss the potential impact of the digital downloading of music, movies, and games on supply chains and retailers. We discuss the success of downloading music and the difficulties retailers such as Wal-Mart have encountered in creating movie download services.

The chapter progresses with in-depth reviews of Starbucks, Best Buy, and Apple. With Starbucks we discuss how they use digital media to "extend their brand" with their base customers. With Best Buy, we review how they are evolving to protect the heart of their business. With Apple, we review the iPod, iTunes, iTunes Store, and the iPhone, and how Apple was able to remake its company through the adoption of the digital supply chain.

Toward the end of the chapter, we take an in-depth look at Media Publisher and how they use digital streaming of video in the business-to-business world. Special emphasis is on content management, content publishing, content distribution, and reporting. We conclude the chapter with a review of how a restaurant chain uses streaming media to enhance their business processes.

Chapter 5: From Sea to Shining Sea: The Changing World of Ocean Container Shipping

The world of ocean container shipping is explored in Chapter 5. The "container" in ocean container shipping is defined, bringing to life the definitions of twenty-foot equivalents or TEUs and forty-foot equivalents or FEUs. A complimentary review of the "ship" sizes is done, with emphasis on the size of the ships and their impact on port unloading capabilities.

The chapter progresses with a review of the work stoppage by the International Longshore and Warehouse Union, the union that represents port workers, and the Pacific Maritime Association at west coast ports in the year 2002. Port congestion is reviewed, along with a bizarre but true personal story regarding forklifts at the Baltimore Inner Harbor. The growth in containerized cargo is discussed as a main driver in port congestion, along with the size restrictions of the Panama Canal. The expansion project of the Panama Canal is reviewed in depth.

Inland international ports are introduced in the chapter as one way the marketplace is responding to port congestion. The need for "secure" containers by the inland international ports is introduced. The pilot programs with "secure technology" in 2004–2005 are reviewed, leading to our definition and forecast for "smart containers." The SensorLogic smart container dashboard is described in detail. The intersection of "smart containers" and transportation management systems is explored, bridging the gap between technology and supply chain management from a business perspective. ZMS Technologies and its suite of TMS applications are reviewed in depth. The summary of the chapter links the marketplace forces with the technologies on the containers, and discusses the need to manage the ocean container supply chain with a sharper financial focus.

Chapter 6: The Warehouse: Obsolete or a Critical Link in the Modern Supply Chain?

Our Chapter 6 is dedicated to the stepchild of supply chain management, the warehouse. We begin the chapter by identifying the hierarchy of costs in the supply chain, with warehousing costs being the smallest component of total landed cost. The implications are that companies will place their best and brightest personnel in the areas of highest economic impact (meaning other areas besides the warehouse).

We describe vendor-managed inventory (VMI) and pay-for-scan in depth. These two programs contribute to products arriving at retailers without passing through traditional warehouses. Historically, the responsibility of store-shelf replenishment resided with the warehouse. Warehouse managers demanded the product flow through the warehouse if they were to be accountable for store-shelf replenishment. With the technologies available today, products can arrive at the store shelf in a multitude of ways. The warehouse manager today is responsible for the store-shelf replenishment regardless of whether or not the product flows through his or her warehouse.

The pay-for-scan and VMI programs are anchored by Warren Buffet's "owner earnings," which are described in detail. This leads us to describe the cash-to-cash cycle and our "four principles of supply chain management."

We progress in our warehouse review with in-depth overviews of order placement, order allocation, and order fulfillment. These reviews provide a basis for our discussion regarding ownership (product) and financial transaction management. One of the underpinnings of sound financial transaction management is remote monitoring, especially remote control. This allows a warehouse manager to trade off higher value activities (manufacturing or transportation) for warehousing costs. If the proper financial systems are in place, warehouse managers can make the proper least landed cost decisions and avoid suboptimal decisions that benefit the warehouse at the expense of the enterprise as a whole.

We summarize by discussing the approach to maximizing the productivity of a "warehouse hour" in terms of the enterprise supply chain. In addition, we close by identifying the need for companies to upgrade the talent in the warehouse to match the store-shelf replenishment responsibilities of the position, not only the warehouse costs of the total landed cost of replenished products.

Chapter 7: Pharmagistics

Our journey continues into the world of pharmaceutical drugs in Chapter 7. We begin the chapter by describing the size of the industry and its economic impact worldwide. We identify the increasing life expectancies of many of the developed countries' populations as a driving force behind an increasing demand for pharmaceutical drugs in the future. In addition, we identify the following forces behind the increasing demand for supply chain professionals in the pharmaceutical industry:

- The number and lengths of discrete supply chains in the value chain of pharmaceutical drugs
- The push to use generic drugs as soon as patent protections expire on branded drugs
- The use of existing drugs for new indications
- The pressure to authenticate drugs and eliminate counterfeit drugs from the legal pharmaceutical drug supply chains

Regarding the fourth bullet point, we delve into the issue of counterfeit drugs. We define what a counterfeit drug is, the size of the problem, and the impact (actual and potential) on human life. The Food and Drug Administration (FDA) and the recommendations of the FDA Counterfeit Drug Task Force Report in 2004 are reviewed in detail. In our review of the first of the seven recommendations, "New Technologies," we discuss the concept of "ePedigree" and its importance to supply chain professionals.

The FDA Counterfeit Drug Task Force 2006 Update is addressed, along with the FDA's "disappointment" regarding the lack of progress with "new technologies." In addition, FDA members now believe that widespread RFID adoption is approximately ten years away because of the maturation issues surrounding RFID technology.

The issue of stolen drugs is addressed through our review of the National Drug Intelligence Center's publication of its National Drug Threat Assessment 2007 report. The four "strategic findings" from this report are covered, along with the good (some states have addressed the mainstream pharmacy issue head-on), the bad (not all states have effective programs), and the ugly (illicit online pharmacies are a breeding ground for both stolen and counterfeit drugs and are not easily addressed by federal or state agencies.) The role of reverse logistics in addressing stolen and counterfeit drugs is covered. Carolina Logistics Services, and its subsidiary, CLS MedTurn, are highlighted for their work in controlling the reverse logistics portion of the pharmaceutical drug supply chain.

The 2004 FDA Counterfeit Task Force is revisited to look at the recommendation for alternative technologies. We introduce Authentix as a company with nano-scale authentic solutions that can address many of the issues surrounding counterfeit and stolen pharmaceutical drugs. Their solutions encompass overt, covert, and forensic markings that, when layered properly with the product and packaging, can help provide a complex barrier to even the most sophisticated "bad guys." We summarize the chapter with our list of six recommendations to address the issues of counterfeit and stolen drugs in the supply chain.

Chapter 8: The Near Future for Technology in Supply Chain Management

We look at the near future for technology in supply chain management in Chapter 8. We begin by identifying the problems within supply chains as primarily cross-functional and inter-enterprise problems. With original equipment manufacturers, transportation asset providers, service providers, and the enterprise's internal functions all participating in moving products through the supply chain, the task to coordinate a tremendous amount of product-related information to flow between the parties becomes very complex. Value-added networks (VANs), such as Sterling Commerce, initially sprang up to provide connectivity between enterprise transactional systems using electronic data interchange (EDI) standards. There is a movement to use XML (extensible markup language) and the Internet to share this needed information.

Collaboration between supply chain partners occurs when a signaling process is used to "signal" demand and trigger supply signals with manufacturers, transport, and distribution providers. This signaling process helps shorten the order-to-cash and cash-to-cash cycles, lowering the costs for all involved. A current issue facing supply chain professionals is the outsourcing of supply functions to other countries such as China. This places a tremendous burden on the use of VAN-based EDI systems and lengthens the order-to-cash and cash-to-cash cycles of the supply chain.

The movement to enterprise resource planning systems helped streamline the intra-enterprise systems of companies throughout the 1990s. These ERP systems did very little for inter-enterprise sharing of information. We believe that the upcoming decade will belong to the technology companies that increase inter-enterprise productivity and solve the never-ending information sharing challenge that outsourcing brings to the table.

There was an earnest effort in the 1990s to tackle this challenge using trading exchanges. Trading exchanges had the right idea but the wrong model. They relied on the use of a common repository of information to share with all supply chain participants. By extending a single instance of an ERP system to several other enterprises, a host of issues regarding data ownership, security, and process flexibility are created.

We believe the use of Web-based services will meet the challenge in the near future. These Web-based applications (e.g., Google Maps) use XML standards and transport protocols to exchange only designated data with client software programs. Supply chain professionals can have their developers access the services from a variety of their supply chain partners and combine these services into composite applications. We believe that Web-based services are part of an evolution to service-oriented architecture (SOA). The flexibility of Web-based services and the ability of SOA to embrace large-scale transaction systems (e.g., order management) are very appealing to supply chain professionals. From a supply chain point of view, Web-based services are clearly appealing. The challenge is to maintain order in a continuously changing environment.

The International Organization for Standardization and commercial and governmental participants are developing standards for how these technologies can be used in a structured fashion to help trading partners perform electronic business in a secure, reproducible way. We call this the "federated enterprise" concept. This concept bases collaboration on a combination of external and internal criteria. Each enterprise maintains its own internal workflow, business procedures, and routines. The federated enterprise architecture creates a framework for managing shared objectives across organizations. Data is not simply replicated; it is shared in the specific context required for the collaborative event to proceed. We discuss the three-step process needed to implement the federated enterprise architecture.

Summary

Supply chain professionals increasingly rely on technology to effectively manage the flow of goods, the flow of information, and the related financial transactions. The question for supply chain professionals to answer is, "Are you relying on the right technologies?" We discuss first "connectivity" technologies (RFID, wireless sensors) in the first three chapters and how these technologies impact the tracking of animals, marine life, and people. We transition our discussion on enabling technologies to compression technologies (new DVDs) and how new technologies can create new supply chains (digital) in Chapter 4. In Chapters 5 and 6, we review the impact of current trends and new technologies in two functional components in the supply chain (ocean container shipping and warehousing). In Chapter 7, we take an in-depth look at the pharmaceutical industry drug supply chain and attempts to thwart counterfeit and stolen drugs from occurring in the supply chain. In Chapter 8, we lay out the near-term future of technology in the supply chain, with special emphasis on the needed architecture for the accelerating extended supply chain.

Throughout the eight chapters, we try to "connect the several dots" that represent the complex world of supply chain management. We provide specific reviews of existing and new technologies, supply chain functional activities, industry supply chains, and enabling technology architectures. All are important for supply chain professionals to "take their game up a notch" and meet the emerging challenges of the global marketplace.

One thing we do know for a fact (other than change is a constant in supply chain management) is that there are no silver bullets when dealing with technology. The path through enabling technologies is a journey—one that involves processes, industry-specific applications, value-propositions to involved stakeholders, and collective learning from past failures and the successes of others. Let us begin our journey with Chapter 1, Radio Frequency Identification—Cure for Cancer or Supplier Curse?

Authors

Fred A. Kuglin is president and CEO of Kuglin, Inc. in Plano, Texas and serves clients at the CXO level in a multitude of industries. Currently he is working with three start-up companies (one in pre-revenue, two in early stage) to secure customers and financing. He recently was the vice-president of business development and vice-president of professional services for a sensor-based, early-stage technology company, where he accounted for the majority of revenues for the company. Kuglin has direct global experience, including in the United Kingdom, multiple EMEA countries, Japan, Singapore, South Korea, Australia, New Zealand, Argentina, Brazil, Uruguay, Mexico, and Venezuela. He is also an advisor to a Dutch-based networking company.

Kuglin holds a bachelor's degree in business administration from the University of Dayton and an MBA in finance from Indiana University. He was a vice-president with Cap Gemini Ernst & Young and a partner with Ernst & Young prior to the acquisition by Cap Gemini. He focused on global supply chain transformation programs specializing in global sourcing, materials management, and the mapping of supply chain operations to overall corporate strategy. Kuglin's responsibilities included the start-up of global practices combining the use of technology-based strategic alliances with account relationships to accelerate the creation of measurable business performance improvement solutions for clients. He was also responsible for Ernst & Young's investments into technology-based start-up companies in CPG, retail and supply chain management.

Kuglin worked for two years as a partner with AT&T Solutions, five years with EDS/AT Kearney (including two years as an ex-pat in Argentina), and nine years with Frito Lay. For Frito Lay, he was responsible for multisite supply chain operations in the upper midwest and southeast. For EDS/AT Kearney, Kuglin started up EDS Consulting Practices in high tech, food, and consumer products. During the ex-pat assignment, he led the acquisition of two South American companies and the start-up of consulting operations in Buenos Aires and Brazil. In addition, Kuglin led the merger of EDS and AT Kearney in Argentina and coled the relaunch of AT Kearney in Brazil postacquisition.

Kuglin has coauthored *Building, Leading, and Managing Strategic Alliances: How to Work Effectively and Profitably with Partner Companies* (AMACOM, 2002) and *The Supply Chain Network @ Internet Speed: Preparing Your Company for the E-Commerce Revolution* (AMACOM, 2000) (a top 25 book on the 1-800-CEO-READ list); and authored *Customer-Centered Supply Chain Management: A Link by Link Guide* (AMACOM, 1998).

He has authored the following articles and white papers:

■ White paper, "Next Generation Media Supply Chain," June 2005
■ White paper, "Harley Davidson: Build-to-Order Excellence," *Nanyang Business Review*, July 2005 (coauthored with Dr. John Slocum and Heidi L. Kuglin)
■ "Building, Leading & Managing Strategic Alliances," *Chief Executive China*, April 2003
■ Cover story, "New Realities of Alliance Partnering," *Financial Executive*, December 2002
■ "The Alliance Advantage," *Business Finance Magazine*, July 2002
■ Editorial, "Next Generation of Supply Chain Management," *Appliance Magazine*, April 2001
■ Host for video production, *Supply Chain Management: Linking Purchasing to Customer Values, Technology and Shareholder Value*, National Association of Purchasing Management, 2001
■ "Logistics," *The Handbook of Cost Management*, 2000
■ "B2B: Building a Networked Supply Chain," iSource Online 1999
■ "Supply Chain Management," *BeyondComputing*, March 1999
■ Contributor, "Satisfying the 21st Century Consumer: Supply Chain Challenges," *Global Sites & Logistics*, May 1999
■ Contributor, "Building a Customer-Centered Supply Chain," *Purchasing Today*, June 1999

Kuglin is a past member of the Dallas Urban League board of directors, having served for several years on the executive committee and as chairman of the technology committee. He was the Ernst & Young and Cap Gemini Dallas Area Diversity Affinity Group Leader and is a certified member of the American Society of Transportation & Logistics. He was also a United Way volunteer, serving as unit chairperson for four agencies. Kuglin was an adjunct professor at Southern Methodist University in Dallas, Texas, for several years. Currently, he is the head usher for St. Mark's, a Catholic church with 24,000 families, and is on the Shoal Creek Homeowners board of directors. Kuglin lives in Plano, Texas, with his wife and two children.

Ray Hood is the CEO of Qumu, Inc. (an on-demand video communications company). Hood is an experienced executive who brings a wealth of experience and leadership that will help Qumu leverage an exciting market opportunity in Web-based services.

He previously built an organization with sales and service operations in fourteen countries, development operations in three countries, and customers in all major markets around the world. Hood serves on the board of directors of OneNetwork, a demand/supply chain solution provider, and on the executive board of advisors at the Southern Methodist University School of Engineering in Dallas, Texas. He is a graduate of the Wharton School of the University of Pennsylvania, and he began his career with Price Waterhouse as a public accountant.

Chapter 1

Radio Frequency Identification: Cure for Cancer or Supplier Curse?

Exciting times await those of us committed to the pursuit of advancements in RFID. Its impact is lauded regularly in mainstream media, with the use of RFID slated to become even more ubiquitous.

From "The History of RFID,"
AIM (Association for Automatic Identification)

If it sounds too good to be true, that's because it is.

Anonymous

Introduction

In June 2003, Wal-Mart asked its top 100 suppliers to place RFID (radio frequency identification) tags on pallets and cases with a deadline of January 2005. Then, in August 2003, Wal-Mart extended this requirement, issuing a mandate requiring all suppliers to put RFID tags on pallets and cases by December 2006. The Wal-Mart supplier community responded to this expensive new requirement with shock, disbelief, and anger.[1]

1

The private, hallway conversations within the Wal-Mart suppliers were very instructive. They revealed that Wal-Mart was trying to track its inventory down to the line-item level to reduce its overall inventory levels, reduce stock-outs, and, most importantly, increase the throughput in its supply chain. The rumor was that Wal-Mart had the objective to increase the product moved through its supply chain by 50 percent with no increase in capital investment. Efficiency gains of this magnitude were unprecedented. In fact, several distribution center equipment providers were panicked, because they had submitted five-year plans that had a "hockey stick" trendline for revenue growth based on expectations of Wal-Mart's explosive growth in facilities. Big changes were certainly in store for the extended Wal-Mart community and a sense of panic spread among some.

Several suppliers told one of us (Fred) that "it was time to start investigating this new technology" so they would not be "left in the dust of their competitors." Fred was in turn shocked at both the suppliers' panic and their belief that RFID technology was radically new.

This leads to a story about Fred's father, Fred T. Kuglin:

In July 2001, Fred T. Kuglin passed away and had a military funeral. During World War II, he was a sergeant in the U.S. Army's 246th Signal Corps and fought in the European theatre. The 246th Signal Corps mission was to go behind enemy lines and set up communications for the advancing Allied troops. This work was very dangerous but necessary, for without communications, the advancing Allied forces would be at a severe disadvantage against the entrenched German army.

Fred T. Kuglin would tell his son stories about a new technology introduced in World War II that would allow the Allied forces to transmit and respond with friendly aircraft. When his unit would receive a response, they knew that the aircraft approaching was friendly. When his unit received no response, they assumed that the approaching aircraft was enemy aircraft. The term "transponder" refers to the "transmit and respond" equipment that used RF to identify friend or foe.

It has been over 60 years since radio frequency technology was used in World War II as an identification method. (So much for the newness of this "new" technology referred to by the supplier.) However, consultants and RFID equipment and tag suppliers seized upon the opportunity to sell "RFID studies" to panicked Wal-Mart suppliers to help educate the suppliers on this new technology being mandated by Wal-Mart. The new gold rush was on, at least for consultants, or so it seemed. Once again, an industry was on the tortured path of inflated expectations about a "new technology" soon to be followed by the inevitable crash of disillusionment (Figure 1.1).

Components of an RFID Solution

The value (or lack of value) in an RFID solution, as with any technology, rests with its proper application and the expected benefits. Before we review the business value

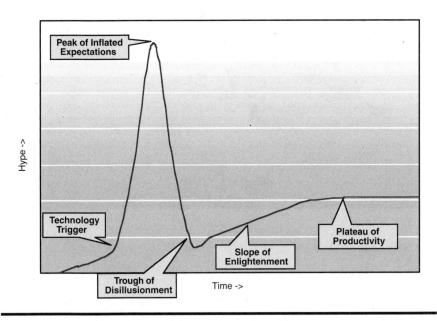

Figure 1.1   The five stages of emerging technology. Source: Ray Hood.

of an RFID solution, it is important to understand the basic terminology, technology, and components that comprise an RFID solution.

Radio frequency identification (RFID) is an automatic identification method, relying on storing and remotely retrieving data using devices called RFID tags or transponders. An *RFID tag* is an object that can be attached to or incorporated into a product, animal, or person for the purpose of identification using radio waves.[2]

The *RFID tag* is created when a microchip is attached to an antenna. The microchip stores an identification number (electronic product code) of the product, animal, or person to which it is attached. The antenna in the RFID tag enables the identification number to be transmitted to a "reader" through radio or electromagnetic waves sent to the RFID tag by the reader.[3] RFID tags come in a variety of "flavors" that we will cover later in this section. Figure 1.2 shows a picture of a variety of Alien Technology tags, ranging from asset tags to item tags.

RFID printers are dual printers, printing standard barcodes and encoding data into an RFID transponder embedded into the label. There are numerous companies that manufacture printers, including Zebra, Avery, Datamax, Printronix, and SATO. The RFID printer prices range from a low of $1,400 up to $8,000, depending on functionality and expected use.[4] Experts agree that Printronix is one of the best RFID printer suppliers in the marketplace. Founded in 1974, Printronix manufactures line matrix printers, RFID and continuous form laser printers, and thermal barcode label printers. Figure 1.3 shows a picture of a Printronix SL5000r RFID printer that produces smart labels and barcodes.

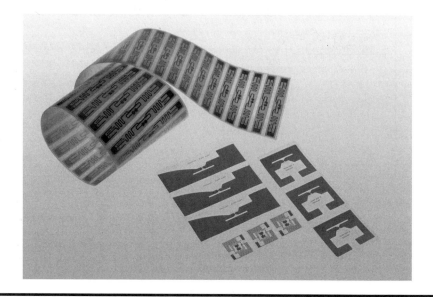

Figure 1.2   Alien Technology tags. Source: Scot Stelter, Director, Reader Product Marketing, Alien Technology.

RFID readers receive the transmitted response from an RFID tag. The tag's identification number is received through the antenna on the reader, converted to a digitized form, and sent to a computer system for processing and association with specific applications. RFID readers are made by Symbol Technologies, Zebra, Intermec, Alien Technology, and several other companies. The RFID reader prices range from several hundred to several thousands of dollars. A typical warehouse application cost would be approximately $1,500 per reader.[5]

Experts also agree that Alien Technology is one of the best suppliers of UHF radio frequency identification products and services to the marketplace. Founded in 1994, Alien Technology is best known for their RFID tags and readers. Figure 1.4 is a picture of an Alien Technology ALR-9900 RFID reader.

Alien Technology also has a reader that combines the reader and the antenna into one box. Figure 1.5 is a picture of the Alien Technology ALR-9650 that provides this combination.

An RFID Tag Is a RFID Tag or Is It?

One senior executive of a consumer products company became frustrated with all the discussions around implementing RFID in his distribution centers. He effectively ended the discussion by saying within earshot of the coauthors, "Go get me some tags, slap and ship them, and make Wal-Mart happy." This was a common refrain heard from Wal-Mart suppliers confused about the costs and benefits of

Figure 1.3   The Printronix SL5000r RFID printer. Source: http://www.printronix .com/partner/.

Figure 1.4   The Alien Technology ALR-9900 RFID reader. Source: Scot Stelter, Director, Reader Product Marketing, Alien Technology.

Figure 1.5   The Alien Technology ALR-9650 reader and antenna. Source: Scot Stelter, Director, Reader Product Marketing, Alien Technology.

Wal-Mart's edict and concerned that they would lose business for noncompliance. It is obvious that he was concurrently receiving advice from consultants and conflicting pressure from his sales organization regarding the volume Wal-Mart represented to his company. However, buying RFID tags is not as easy as going shopping at Wal-Mart. Not all tags are created equal. There are three types of RFID tags: passive, semi-active, and active.

Passive RFID tags basically have no internal power. When a reader sends electromagnetic waves to the passive RFID tag, it generates a minute amount of electrical current in the tag itself. This small amount of electrical current is enough for the circuit in the tag to power up or "wake up" and send a response to the reader. Without its own power supply, a passive RFID tag can be quite small (.15 mm × .15 mm). However, the read range for passive RFID tags is only a few feet. The lowest cost passive RFID tags currently in use by Wal-Mart and other organizations are approximately 10 to 15 cents each.[6] While this sounds cheap, imagine the cost of generating the tags and applying them to every single item shipped into the Wal-Mart supply chain.

Passive RFID tags become *semi-passive RFID tags* when they contain their own power source for use in its internal control circuitry. This capability may be used to acquire and/or store additional information. Semi-passive tags do not have their own power supply to transmit a response back to a reader.

Active RFID tags have their own internal power source to generate an outgoing signal or response to a reader. Frequently this power source is in the form of a battery, and allows active tags to transmit at higher power levels. This is important when

Figure 1.6   The Alien Technology "squiggle tag." Source: Scot Stelter, Director, Reader Product Marketing, Alien Technology.

RFID tags are being used in tough environments where the RF signal has to pass some distance or through water or metal. Some active tags have larger memories, contain sensors for the collection and storage of some information, and can be the size of an average-sized coin. Active RFID tags have a read range of up to 279 ft, or 85 m. The more advanced active tags sell for approximately $25.[7]

More than 70% of the shipments into Wal-Mart use the "squiggle" passive tag. It is very recognizable by its shape. Figure 1.6 is a picture of the Alien Technology "squiggle tag."

Then There Are the Frequencies to Consider...

RFID tags and readers must communicate using the same frequency. There are four commonly used frequencies in an RFID solution. These frequencies are "low" (~125 kHz), "high" (13.56 MHz), "ultrahigh" or UHF (902 to 928 MHz), and microwave (2.45 GHz.)

Low frequency tags are cheaper, use less power, and more easily penetrate non-metal substances. The tags must be very close to the readers. Ultrahigh frequency tags usually have higher ranges, use more power, and can transmit data faster. However, the UHF frequency tags do not penetrate troublesome materials as well as low frequency tags and must have a direct, clear path to a reader.

To compound the issue, the major trading blocs around the world have not agreed on a common UHF spectrum for RFID. Europe uses 868 MHz, the United States uses 915 MHz, and Japan is about to open up 960 MHz. There is a global commerce initiative (called EPC global) to get the countries around the world to agree on common frequencies and output.[8] (Based on the performance of other international standards organizations related to supply chains in the last 20 years, we will not hold our breath on this happening in our lifetime.)

How the RFID System Works...or Tries to Work

(For our example, we will assume that only full-case quantities are being shipped from a supplier to a RFID-mandated retailer.)

Either a supplier receives product from a "tier" or another supplier, or its warehouse receives product from its own production line. In the case of product received

Frequency Summary Table

Frequency	Range	Application
Low frequency		
125–148 kHz	3 Feet	Animal and pet tracking
High frequency		
13.56 MHz	3 Feet	Smart cards, softlines
Ultra-high frequency		
915 MHz	25 Feet	Carton, pallet, trailer and container tracking
Microwave		
2.45 GHz	100 Feet	Road toll collection

Source: Fred A. Kuglin.

from another supplier, RFID tags are placed on the cases (and possibly the pallet) upon receipt from the transport company. In the situation of an onsite manufacturing plant, RFID tags are placed on the cases at the packaging station just prior to entering the warehouse. Two RFID readers are usually placed on either side of the receiving doors to pick up the responses from the RFID tags as they enter the warehouse.

The warehouse management system (WMS) assigns a "put-away" location to the product based on a combination of random-access storage and velocity of through-put factors. The product is then placed in the specified location in the warehouse for onsite storage, passing by two more readers placed for full pallet or case inventory.

When the order pick lanes are in need of replenishment, the warehouse worker is directed by the WMS system to retrieve the pallet of product and reposition the cases to the appropriate order pick lane. The two put-away readers pick up the removal of the pallet and cases, while two more readers at the pick lane pick up the receipt of the pallet/cases.

When another warehouse "picks" to an order from a retailer, the cases are placed on a pick belt to be sent to the appropriate loading door. The cases go through another set of readers and are sorted and diverted to the appropriate loading door based on the electronic order fill.

If everything goes smoothly, then the cases are loaded onto a truck, going through two more sets of readers on the sides of the loading dock door. The shipping manifest is closed out, and an invoice is generated for the retailer or the inventory is transferred to the retail store by the retailer's distribution center.

The RFID responses picked up by the readers are digitized and sent to the internal systems for association with the order and shipping manifest.

Now Comes the Hard Part

In our example, there were multiple readers in the warehouse picking up multiple signals from pallets and cases. This is called reader collision. A typical Wal-Mart distribution center ships over 300,000 cases of product a day! The chances of readers picking up the same signal or response from a case or pallet are very high.

Some companies have implemented what is called time division multiple access, or TDMA. This is where different readers read while others are "asleep," and vice versa. If this staggering of read times does not work, then a system needs to be set up to eliminate multiple or unnecessary reads. This type of system can be very complex.

In addition, imagine a pallet of 64 cases of product. A reader will receive 64 signals or responses plus one from the pallet. This is called tag collision. Some companies have designed systems for tags to respond at variable rates to minimize tag collision.

Misreads Anyone?

Supply chain professionals have it tough enough working with their information technology (IT) counterparts to manage tag and reader collisions. Perhaps a more daunting task is for these professionals to implement an RFID solution and deal with metal and water.

Metals are sometimes friends but usually enemies of RFID signals. When the readers send out a signal to an RFID tag and a response is generated, chances are these cases are moving in a warehouse. These responses have to be directed back at the reader in order for the reader to "pick up" the response. Needless to say, there is a lot of metal in a warehouse. From the storage racks to the pick belts to the sorter and diverter trays—there is metal everywhere. If the tags are not placed in *perfect* position for the reader to pick up the signal response, the response may be bouncing off metal. (Ever wonder what happens to all of these responses bouncing around the warehouse?)

Water is another enemy of RFID signals. However, as metal reflects and diverts RFID tag responses, water absorbs these responses. Initial RFID tests with cattle (and people) revealed that the water make-up of cattle and people absorbed these signals and prevented them from making their way to the readers.

There are several system integrators who "brag" that they can help clients achieve a 94% to 96% "read rate" in their warehouses. Initially, this percentage looks terrible. However, with tag collision, reader collision, metal everywhere, misplaced tags on cartons, and water-based substances sometimes being shipped, a 94% to 96% read rate may be "bragging territory." Unfortunate for RFID backers, simple barcode systems currently achieve accuracy rates far higher than RFID systems.

Bragging to the CFO...?

Bragging about a 94% to 96% read rate from a technical standpoint is one thing. Bragging about the financial implications of a 4% to 6% misread rate is another thing altogether.

As stated earlier, the average Wal-Mart warehouse ships 300,000+ cases of product a day, 24 hours a day, 7 days a week. A 5% misread rate means that 15,000 cases per day per Wal-Mart warehouse will be "misreads." Of course, this is why Wal-Mart demands 100% read rates from their suppliers. As such, the burden of misreads is shifted to the supplier.

The challenge of misreads is compounded by the nature of the warehouse operations. In a pharmaceutical or movie studio DVD warehouse, the automated pick lanes operate in number of items picked *per second*. It is not uncommon for a pharmaceutical warehouse (usually a third-party logistics provider or contracted manufacturer) to ship over 100 million "items" per year, or roughly 2 million per week. A 5% misread rate means that the warehouse personnel must deal with 100,000 misreads a week, or 20,000 per day! If they are only placing RFID tags on cases, then the number of misreads drops to a number from several hundred to a few thousand per day.

When a misread occurs, the item or case is diverted to what is affectionately called "the jackpot lane." This area is usually outfitted with a computer and access to the WMS, an RFID printer, and a smaller (sometimes handheld) RFID reader unit. The lucky warehouse worker assigned to "the jackpot lane" is responsible for two critical tasks. The first assignment is to make sure that the order is back-filled to reach a 100% order-fill rate before the shipment is sent to the retailer. The second assignment is to both physically and electronically return the item to the pick lanes. In high velocity warehouses, there are usually two or more full-time workers that work full-time in the jackpot lane.

The misread RFID tags are for the most part discarded. New RFID tags are printed before the product is placed back in the customer order or back into inventory.

Costs in the CFO's Cost/Benefit Analysis

Let us go back to the Wal-Mart distribution center. If every case shipped to a Wal-Mart store has an RFID tag, the cost to the Wal-Mart suppliers (assuming 15 to 20 cents per tag) would be $45,000 to $60,000 per day, or $16.4 to $21.8 million per year for only the RFID tags! There are approximately 112 distribution centers in North America.[9] The RFID tag total alone is approximately $2.6 billion, or 1.375% of the estimated $200 billion Wal-Mart spends with its suppliers. If we add in the cost of the readers, the edge servers, the extra printers, the added warehouse personnel, etc., the RFID program total for the suppliers may rise to 1.5% of the $200 billion, or $3 billion. It is little wonder that RFID tag manufacturers, RFID printer and reader manufacturers, systems integrators, and RFID software companies sprang up like weeds after a good spring rain. However, the "CFO effect" was soon to bring everyone back to fiscal reality.

Benefits in the CFO's Cost/Benefit Analysis and Supplier Resistance

The costs associated with implementing an RFID system are real and implementation is hard. Initially most of these costs fall on the suppliers. In contrast, the benefits for Wal-Mart are well documented. For RFID-tagged items, Wal-Mart states that it reduced out of stocks by 8% worldwide and can re-supply three times faster. In addition, Wal-Mart stores can prioritize the unloading of trucks based on the highest priority items to be unloaded.[10] However, the benefits for the Wal-Mart suppliers (and Department of Defense suppliers, the other monster entity mandating usage) remain elusive.

For some suppliers, implementation of an RFID system required upgrading of their IT infrastructures. Of course, consultants and systems integrators rushed in with their RFID business case programs, eager to identify the hard benefits of implementing the RFID systems. Unfortunately, in many cases, the biggest benefit for suppliers was the *avoidance* of losing Wal-Mart as a customer!

Suppliers do lose out when a stock-out occurs on a retailer's store shelf. In addition, when suppliers work with retailers in a "pay-for-scan" format, the suppliers *have* to know when and where their inventory is located until it is scanned upon purchase by a customer or returned by the retailer.

Some suppliers have successfully pushed back against Wal-Mart and have limited the RFID system implementations to full-case quantities. The movie studios, for example, ship over 1 billion DVDs into the marketplace, with approximately one third going to Wal-Mart stores. The tag costs alone would be $200 million. A 20-cent RFID tag represents a 2% surcharge on an average $10 DVD (non-new release) at store door value, or a 4% reduction in margin for the movie studios. There are alternatives (digital supply chain for downloading movies), but these will be discussed in another chapter.

RFID Applications with Some Success…Maybe

During a tour of three automotive plants, two Japanese transplants and one American automotive manufacturer, we observed RFID in use in several areas. RFID tags were placed on totes and bins coming in from third-party logistics providers (3pls). The totes and bins were received on pallets. As the pallets were unloaded from the truck, they passed by RFID readers set up on either side of the receiving doors.

In two of the three plants, the plant's inbound receiving warehousemen were scanning labels on the totes and bins as well. When we asked the warehousemen why they were scanning labels with RFID tags and readers, they gave the same answer. The "read rates" were not 100% accurate, so they still used labels and scanned every tote and bin. (In one case, there appeared to be 12 rows of 9 totes, or 108 totes on a pallet. Other than a misapplied RFID tag, the reason for the misreads appeared to be reader collision.) The accounts payable personnel demanded accurate receiving records, so the warehousemen used the old reliable method of scanning the barcode on each tote.

We proceeded to ask the inbound receiving warehouse managers why they still used the RFID tags and readers. One manager said it was too labor intensive to rip everything out. Another manager said the 3pls and the tier one suppliers paid for the hardware, and as such, they were free, so why do anything with them. In all cases, the RFID receiving documentation was never really used or reconciled to anything.

In one manufacturing plant, an RFID tag was placed on an empty part transport trolley used in their Kanban system. When the empty part transport trolley moved past an RFID reader, the reader would "read" the RFID tag. The reading of the RFID tag on the empty part transport trolley was a replenishment signal to the parts inventory system and the 3pl. To our amazement, the use of RFID with the empty part transport trolley actually worked very well! There was widespread resistance to expanding the use of RFID to replace the card system, but there was widespread acceptance of RFID with the empty part trolley for replenishment signals.

One area that RFID was deployed in all three plants was with the finished vehicles. As finished vehicles came off the assembly line, RFID tags and barcodes were placed on them. RFID readers were placed on either side of the door leading from the manufacturing plants to the outside parking lots. As the vehicles passed the readers, the tags were read by the RFID readers. When the driver would exit the vehicle, a lot management person would scan the barcode on the vehicle. The RFID tag was used to determine finished vehicles for manufacturing production purposes. The scanning of the barcodes on the vehicles was performed to transfer the finished vehicle from the manufacturing plant inventory to "transport."

The transport groups managed the finished vehicle lots adjacent to the manufacturing plants. Finished vehicles parked in these lots are waiting for an allocation to a specific dealer or on a transport vehicle (railcar or truck trailer.) With all three manufacturing plants, there were hundreds of finished vehicles on these lots.

All three manufacturing plants and their finished vehicles lot management partners had access to sophisticated lot management systems. None of the three ever used their systems to identify specific locations for specific vehicles. All three used their systems to verify they were in receipt of specific vehicles (using the vehicle identification number, or VIN) or to "ship" a finished vehicle when it was loaded on a railcar or truck trailer.

There was logic—albeit a little twisted—to why the lot management system was not used. The driver from the manufacturing plant to the lot management person would travel all of 100 to 200 feet before turning over the finished vehicle to the lot management person. The manufacturing plant took credit for the vehicle when it passed the RFID reader. No more action was needed by the driver. The lot management person would scan the vehicle, look for any visible defects, and have another driver take it "to an open space" on the finished vehicle transport lot. Sometimes, when the finished vehicle was built to a specific order, the finished vehicle would be tagged and sent to a special holding area. The drivers who took the vehicles from the manufacturing plant to the finished vehicle lot were literally running back from the finished vehicle lots to the manufacturing plant. There was no time for the drivers to update the lot management system.

The finished vehicle lot management personnel did have some manual systems in place. One plant had areas of the finished vehicle lots identified by day of production. Another plant had the finished vehicles parked by color (or tried to park the finished vehicles by color.) This appeared to work 90% of the time. The third manufacturing plant separated their lot by railcar and truck trailer. The use of railcars always had priority because of the cost differential between rail and truck. This seemed to work pretty well, except for the use of finished vehicles in the rail yard to fill specific truck trailers and complete a load.

Our puzzlement centered primarily on the answers to the question of why RFID readers were not placed at strategic locations throughout the finished vehicle transport lots to track specific vehicles. One person said the readers would not work in inclement weather. Another person said the tag read rates were too low (despite the manufacturing plant using them to track finished vehicles exiting the plant). The most puzzling answer was the one on cost. This person said they were only given so much per vehicle to park and load the finished vehicle on a railcar or truck trailer. They did not have the budget for RFID tags and readers. At the same time, this person's transport group had several people running around with barcode scanners looking for specific vehicles to place on specific railcars and truck trailers to complete loads and meet the associated dispatch times! The labor cost alone for these people would easily justify the RFID tags and readers.

On a related note, each of the finished vehicle transport groups averaged "losing" two to six finished vehicles per year. The majority of the "lost" finished vehicles were eventually "found" and determined to be mis-shipped. For these mis-shipped finished vehicles, there was a cost to reposition the finished vehicle to its proper destination (estimated to be $350 to $1,000). For the few truly "lost" finished vehicles, the cost was the inventory value of the finished vehicle (or several thousands of dollars.) The cost avoidance of mis-shipping finished vehicles and losing the occasional finished vehicle could easily cover the costs associated with expanding the use of RFID.

The use of RFID to account for finished vehicle production could be considered a partial success. In our opinion, the use of RFID with finished vehicles will be considered a complete success when the automotive companies do away with their barcode systems.

RFID Applications That Make Good Common— and Business—Sense

Numerous other RFID applications are in use today. For example, the public transit systems of New York, Moscow, Hong Kong, and Singapore, as well as numerous toll roads, use RFID smartcards tied to credit or debit cards.

Philips in particular is very active in RFID transportation projects, using its MIFARE technology. In Brazil alone, Philips is involved with more than 60 transport ticketing projects that total 10 to 12 million RFID transport cards a year.[11] Brazil is a good market for deploying RFID transport cards, with São Paulo being a model city for successful deployment.

São Paulo is the world's third largest city, with a metropolitan population exceeding 18 million people. In São Paulo State, the population exceeds 40 million people, the equivalent of the population of Argentina and more than double the population of Chile.[12] People in São Paulo rely heavily on mass transportation, in particular, trains, underground subways, and buses.

Philips, working with systems integrators Prodata and Digicon, have developed an RFID fare card called the Bilhete Único ("single ticket"). Passengers can use the Bilhete Único card to travel by bus, train, and underground subway throughout all São Paulo.[13]

Rio de Janeiro is not far behind. Philips and Prodata have developed the RioCard to be used on all city buses, minibuses, and the local ferry network. Other Brazilian cities such as Fortaleza, Manaus, and Cuiabá are pursuing deployments (albeit on a much smaller scale) of their own. The success of the RFID transportation projects has caused Brazil to review using RFID technology in a number of other applications. These applications include electronic passports, access control for government sites, livestock tracking, smart labels in supply chain management, and student identification cards. The student ID cards are planned for the tracking of attendance and the tracking of students on school buses.[14]

The North Texas Tollway Authority (NTTA) has an extensive network of toll roads throughout the North Texas (Dallas–Ft. Worth) area. Officially, the NTTA is a political subdivision of the State of Texas under Chapter 366 of the Transportation Code. It is empowered to acquire, construct, maintain, repair, and operate turnpike projects; to raise capital for construction projects through the issuance of Turnpike

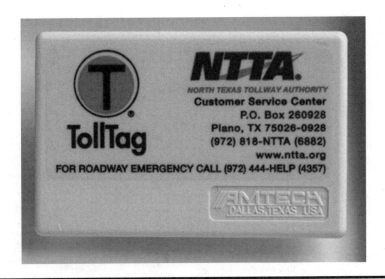

Figure 1.7   The North Texas Tollway Authority TollTag. Source: NTTA, Plano, Texas.

Revenue Bonds; and to collect tolls to operate, maintain, and pay debt service on those projects.[15]

The NTTA uses an RFID-based toll tag for its toll roads (Figure 1.7). These toll tags record the usage and charge a credit or debit card of the toll tag user.

There are multiple users of toll roads. Current NTTA operations allow for the mixed use of attendant or change-provided lanes, exact change lanes, and express lanes for toll tag users. Figure 1.8 depicts this mixed-use toll booth operation.

The application of technology has become so pervasive that the majority of toll road users are toll tag users. The NTTA is transforming their toll booth operations to toll tag operations only (Figure 1.9). The savings are significant. The users of the toll roads benefit from lower fares and reduced congestion around toll booths. The NTTA benefits from reduced labor at the toll booths, reduced labor in the handling of money received at the toll booths, and reduced risk in both the handling of money and having toll booth operators in harm's way of errant motorists.

Beyond transport solutions, other successful RFID implementations have involved ski resorts, airline baggage handling, apparel and pharmaceutical item tracking, cars and car keys, truck and trailer tracking in shipping yards, and animal and human implants. In most of these cases, the RFID tag is placed directly in front of an RFID reader for a very high read rate of the signal response.

Human implants with RFID tags are gaining in popularity in the marketplace. In the case of an Indiana-based start-up, an RFID tag is sprayed on the implant at the time of surgery. The RFID tag contains the implant identification number, procedure date, and other patient record information (Figure 1.10). Once the implant

Figure 1.8   Mixed-use toll booth operation. Source: NTTA, Plano, Texas.

Figure 1.9   NTTA TollTag only toll booth. Source: NTTA, Plano, Texas.

is set, but prior to the closure of the patient, the RFID reader "reads" the data from the RFID tag to ensure readability. Some medical facilities immediately transmit these data to a "patient record management system."

The value proposition of using RFID tags on implants is centered on the avoidance of malpractice lawsuits. According to one leading hospital in the upper

Figure 1.10   A human hand with an RFID chip implant. Source: http://en.wikipedia .org/wiki/RFID.

midwest of the United States, the number one reason for malpractice claims associated with implants is the claim of the wrong implant being used during surgery. If the implants had an RFID tag, a quick scan of the implant by an RFID reader would confirm or dispel the suspicion that the wrong implant was used during surgery. Without the RFID tag, the only way to tell if the wrong implant was used during surgery is to open the patient up and visually inspect the implant!

Back to Wal-Mart

In February 2007, *The Wall Street Journal* ran an article entitled, "Wal-Mart's Radio-Tracked Inventory Hits Static."[16] The article summarized Wal-Mart's RFID program as moving very slowly, largely due to vendor reluctance because they see limited value thus far. "As Wal-Mart searches for an answer to its rising costs, suppliers are saying RFID isn't it," the *Journal* wrote. "Wal-Mart has pushed its suppliers to use exotic radio-activated tags to chop labor and inventory costs anew. But tests using the tags aren't showing any savings, and suppliers forced to invest in the relatively expensive technology are grumbling."[17] This article shot a bullet right into the heart of the RFID industry. Its spokespeople were livid.

For those people in the consumer products and retail industries, the article contained relatively old news. Most of the senior executives we know have resigned themselves to consider the cost of RFID implementations as a cost to do business with Wal-Mart. They incorporate this cost into the cost of their products sold to Wal-Mart when and where they can do so. These same executives believe there will be a day when RFID will produce the benefits it was hyped to generate earlier this decade. However, they believe they won't be around when the day arrives! As predictable as the responses were from the senior executives, the responses of RFID advocates were surprising.

In an article in *SupplyChainDigest* dated February 22, 2007, the writer stated the following: "Executives at hundreds of consumer goods companies, including CEOs, will read this article, and it may likely embolden those dragging their feet on adoption and wait still longer."[18] We believe this statement may be true for the few CEOs who are relatively incompetent. However, most CEOs and senior executives of consumer goods companies that have Wal-Mart as their customer are very close to Wal-Mart and its RFID program. In most cases, Wal-Mart is the "personal account" of the most senior executive. Senior executives are also highly skilled in analyzing the costs and benefits of new programs. For the majority of these CEOs, *The Wall Street Journal* article will not replace a positive or negative cost/benefit analysis for determining the adoption rate of RFID technology. It will most certainly not replace the professional relationship these companies have with Wal-Mart.

The article also stated, "As always, we reiterate *SupplyChainDigest*'s stance that RFID is an excellent technology that over time will largely replace barcodes."[19] We believe that RFID technology may in time replace barcodes. However, we also believe there may be other technologies that are more effective in producing measurable business value to companies in the immediate future than waiting for RFID technology to mature.

Mark Roberti, the founder and editor of *RFID Journal*, was alarmed by *The Wall Street Journal* article but was almost "spot-on" in his assessment. He stated in his article on February 19, 2007 that the article "stories like this—and we've seen many—can have a chilling effect on RFID adoption."[20] He went on to identify the positive results of RFID at Wal-Mart, including the reduction of stock-outs by as much as 60% on some fast-moving items. He also referred to benefits derived by Proctor & Gamble and Kimberly-Clark in the tracking of promotional items. Roberti stressed the importance of deploying RFID intelligently, and to look for ways of how and where it can deliver value today. This way, companies will not abandon RFID and miss the benefits when RFID technology matures in the future. We agree with Roberti's comments, yet also believe supply chain professionals must seek out other technologies as RFID matures.

Conclusion

For the supply chain professional, a moving asset (independent of the RFID reader) will have to rely on a different technology (potentially sensors) to produce benefits that far exceed costs. In the meantime, our CEO may be smart after all. It may be wise to follow the CFO's lead and implement the bare minimum to comply with a Wal-Mart or DoD mandate until the cost per RFID tag drops down to low single digits.

There are a number of lessons to learn from RFID in retail.

The Wal-Mart mandate is yet another illustration of the hype of new technology and the imbalance of benefits between parties of the supply chain holding back effective implementation. Wal-Mart's mandate can be considered a partial success inside of Wal-Mart and a failure outside the organizational boundaries of Wal-Mart. In our opinion, Wal-Mart's mandate has held back more appropriate uses of the technology by focusing industry resources too heavily on Wal-Mart.

When new technology is introduced into a complex industry like the retail supply chain it is important to ask the question: Qui bono? Who benefits? In the Wal-Mart case the benefits clearly accrued were mostly to them. In fact, Wal-Mart's warehouse labor savings alone, because RF tags (unlike barcodes) are "nonline of sight," are worth hundreds of millions of dollars each year. The benefits to the suppliers, on the other hand, are harder to quantify and further in the future. This imbalance of benefits doomed this effort from the beginning.

What were the alternatives? Existing barcode technology already in use for 30 years along with standards for barcode labels (Standard Shipping Container Code and Serialized Shipping Container Code, SSCC-14 and SSCC-18, respectively) could yield many of the benefits of RFID but were rarely fully utilized by the industry. Why not? The reasons are fights over standards, requirements for change to process, and other barriers. So why did Wal-Mart and industry pundits think that adding complex new technology such as RFID tags along with the readers and the integration to other systems would be better? The answer is that any objective analysis at the time of the mandate would clearly have concluded that RFID, while clearly advantageous, would be a decade or longer adoption process. In addition, the initial focus should have been on high value and high shrink items, while the technology gracefully matured before forcing suppliers to use it with cases of bananas and pallets of peas.

We now continue to ride the hype curve. We are past RFID's "inflated expectations" climbing out of the "trough of disillusionment." Now the real work climbing up the long "slope of enlightenment" begins.

Notes

1. http://www.rfidjournal.com/article/articleview/539/1/1/, August 18, 2003, and numerous conversations with Fred Kuglin at RFID conferences in late 2003 and 2004.
2. http://en.wikipedia.org/wiki/RFID.
3. http://www.rfidjournal.com/article/articleview/207, "How Does an RFID System Work?" and discussions by Fred Kuglin with Symbol Technologies Sales representative June, 2007.
4. http://www.nextag.com/rfid-printers/search-html.
5. http://www.nextag.com/rfid-reader, and personal experiences by Ray Hood and Fred Kuglin.
6. http://www.mmh.com/article/CA6574261.html.

7. http://www.rfidlabeling.com/tag_types.html.

8. http://www.epcglobalinc.org/home.

9. http://walmartstores.com/FactsNews/NewsRoom/8326.aspx.

10. http://networkworld.com/news/2008/091508-wal-mart-rfid.html?page=2,3.

11. http://www.nxp.com/infocus/otm/success/otm81/brazil/.

12. http://travel.nationalgeographic.com/places/cities.city_saopaulo.html, and http://www.saopaulo.sp.gov.br/ingles/.

13. http://www.nxp.com/news/identification/articles/otm81/brazil/.

14. http://www.nxp.com/infocus/otm/success/otm81/brazil/.

15. http://www.ntta.org/AboutUs/Who/; "Who We Are."

16. McWilliams, Gary. "Wal-Mart's Radio-Tracked Inventory Hits Static," *The Wall Street Journal*, February 18, 2007, D06.

17. Ibid.

18. http://www.scdigest.com/assets/newsViews/08-02-22-1.cfm?cid=908&ctype=content. *SupplyChainDigest*, News and Views, February 22, 2007.

19. Ibid.

20. http://www.rfidjournal.com/article/articleprint/3051/-1/1. February 19, 2007.

Chapter 2

Wireless Sensors: The Value-Based World beyond Radio Frequency Identification

Knowledge signifies things known. Where there are no things known, there is no knowledge. Where there are no things to be known, there can be no knowledge.

Frances Wright, Course of Popular Lectures, lecture 4 (1829)

As we know,
There are known knowns.
There are things we know we know.
We also know
There are known unknowns.
That is to say
We know there are some things
We do not know.
But there are also unknown unknowns,
The ones we don't know
We don't know.

Donald Rumsfeld, Secretary of Defense,
Department of Defense news briefing, February 12, 2002

Introduction

The limitations of radio frequency identification (RFID) technology in its application to supply chains are creating a "value barrier" between RFID costs and the
associated RFID benefits. As a result of the limited functionality (IDs only), high
cost of deployment of readers, and lack of enterprise systems to take advantage of
the technology, few product suppliers and transport providers share in the benefits
that some retailers are seeing. The placement of sensors into active RFID tags is a
good first step to address these limitations and starts to break down this value barrier, at least for some participants.

A sensor is a device that receives and responds to a signal or stimulus.[1] It can be
further defined as a device that measures a physical quantity and converts it into a
signal that can be read by an observer or an instrument. Sensors can be either direct
indicating (e.g., a mercury thermometer or electric meter) or are paired with an indicator (an analog to digital converter, a computer and/or a device with a computer chip,
and a display) so that the value sensed becomes readable to humans.[2]

There are numerous types of sensors. The types of sensors include, but are not
limited to, thermal, electromagnetic, mechanical, chemical, optical, ionizing radiation, non-ionizing radiation, acoustic, motion, distance, and many others.[3] Sensors
are used in industries ranging from process (e.g., food) to industrial machinery
and from oil and gas to electronics. It is hard to imagine going through our daily
activities without coming into contact with a sensor application. In addition, there
are "logical" sensors. A logical sensor is a sensor whose data is based on data from
one or more sensors, possibly involving one or more mathematical algorithms.[4] An
example of such a sensor is one that receives a temperature reading in Celsius and
reports the temperature in Fahrenheit.

In recent times, some experts point to the use of sensors in the motion picture
industry in the 1950s as the first application of sensors. However, in 1898 Emil
Wiechert of Göttingen, Germany, introduced a seismograph with a viscously damped
pendulum as a sensor. Wiechert's first seismograph was a horizontal-pendulum instrument, which recorded photographically. Wiechert then built a mechanically record-
ing seismograph. For a sensor, he used an inverted pendulum stabilized by springs
that was free to oscillate in any direction horizontally. The seismograph was completed between 1899–1900.[5] Was Wiechert's seismograph the first use of a "sensor"?
Engineers and historians can date pressure sensors back to the 1600s and temperature sensors to the 1700s. Some people believe that weight sensors were used in the
B.C. era.[6] It is safe to assume that sensors have been in existence for a long time.

The roles of sensors in supply chains can be directly linked to two different
types of applications—sensors on fixed assets and sensors on mobile assets. Both
have their own distinct value propositions.

Sensors on fixed assets have been in use for decades. Sensors have been used on
automotive assembly lines, on industrial pumps, on forklifts, in warehouse racking,
on automatic palletizers, on packaging machines, and even on weight scales on our

nations highways. As mentioned earlier, these sensors are usually paired with an indicator to convert what they are sensing to a human readable form. In our homes, sensors are used in thermostats to "read" room temperatures, in water heaters to "read" water temperatures, and in smoke alarms to "read" the presence of particles in the air. In fixed assets in the supply chain, sensors "read" weight, density, open spaces in storage racks, interference behind forklifts, and the entering or exiting of trucks on a warehouse or trucking depot lot.

The information from sensors on fixed assets is usually sent to enterprise systems through a communications "landline." A landline is a communications line that travels through a solid medium, either a metal wire or optical fiber. A landline is also a very secure form of communications, as it cannot be intercepted by a receiver without physical access to the line. The term landline is also used to describe a connection between two points that consists of a dedicated physical cable, as opposed to an always-available private link that is actually implemented as a circuit in a wider switched system (usually the public telephone network). Sometimes the terms "fixed line" and "main line" are used interchangeably with "landline."[7]

Fixed-Asset Sensors, RFID, and Barcodes

Sensors, RFID technologies, and barcodes have coexisted for years in the supply chain. For example, in the automotive plant, sensors were placed on the assembly line to assist the use of robotics. They are also used to measure the "fill-rates" of totes and bins in the Japanese *Kanban* manufacturing system (although some manufacturing plants have a tough time getting rid of the "cards" in their *Kanbans*). As we discussed in Chapter 1, RFID tags and barcodes have been placed on these same totes and bins to help locate and route the totes from the time they are filled until the time they are in need of replenishment. They have also been successfully placed on the associated empty part transport trolleys to signal the need for replenishment.

In the food processing business, sensors have been used to help clean raw materials and separate debris before processing, to fill (but not overfill) packages through sophisticated statistical weighing machines, to properly rotate automated palletizing machines, and to sense the need to replenish production supplies when supplies drop below the minimum acceptable supply levels. Barcodes have been used to track the product from packaging and palletization through receipt, storage, and shipment activities in the warehouse.

Value Proposition Examples—Fixed-Asset Sensors in a Plant Environment

In automotive assembly plants, robots were outfitted with sensors to detect "empty spaces" in the assembly lines. Each empty space represents one lost unit of production. The data from these sensors is transmitted through landlines to in-house systems used by plant operations. Alarms are issued when the appropriate in-house systems process the data from the robots on the empty spaces in the assembly line. The notifications to the appropriate people are then sent to correct the problem creating the empty spaces, thus minimizing the number of lost production units. One lost unit of production per hour can amount to tens of thousands of dollars. The authors believe the real value proposition is to reverse this "empty space" notification process. The supplier or transport driver should send an alert to the in-house systems and the assembly line robots to "re-plan" the assembly schedule when a shortage of material is known. It is absolutely too late to effectively respond if the assembly plant lets the assembly line robot be the first line of "alerts" when material shortages occur.

Food processing companies have used sensors in bag and box fill machines for years. The more sophisticated machines use a combination of optical and weight sensors to scan finished products and weigh multiple combinations before directing these combinations to the appropriate bag or box. Before these "stat weighing" machines were used, it was a common industry practice to over-fill boxes or bags by an average of 10%. (There are significant government regulations and penalties for consumer companies to "under-fill" stated weights and/or volumes on packaging labels.) After the introduction of these box and bag fill machines with optical and weight sensors, the average over-fill dropped from 10% to 1%.[8]

This drop in over-fill may not appear significant to some readers. However, for example, for Kellogg's selling over 1 billion boxes of corn flakes or for Frito-Lay selling over 1 billion bags of corn chips a year, the savings is over 90 million boxes of corn flakes or bags of corn chips. If the store-door value of a box of corn flakes or a bag of corn chips is $1.50, then each company just saved the equivalent of $135 million by reducing their over-fills. In addition, the savings in spending associated with the capital assets required to fill and handle the unnecessary 90 million boxes or bags of product, from warehouses to manufacturing plants to delivery trucks, is significant as well.

Back to the Wal-Mart and Department of Defense Challenges

In Chapter 1, we discussed the hallway "chatter" among the suppliers to Wal-Mart about Wal-Mart wanting to increase the amount of throughput through its distribution centers by 50% without any increase in spending on facilities. The U.S. Department of Defense wants to track all shipments in trailers and containers *and* to have physical evidence of unauthorized entries into these assets. In both cases, the need is to track the product and the trailers or containers from the time the product enters the supply chain until the time the product is placed on the store shelf or arrives at the final secure destination. This includes multiple parties handling the product and at times the responsibility for the product changing hands as well. This scenario is far beyond the fixed assets inside the four walls of a distribution center or production plant, and involves the use of mobile assets.

If the world evolved around a manufacturing plant or a warehouse, sensors with wireline communications and RFID technology might be all that companies need to efficiently manage their supply chains. However, products do move throughout their supply chains. Some products move very quickly. It takes less than four days to convert corn and oil into corn chips and get the chips to store shelves. It takes only hours to convert flour, water, and yeast into bread and get the bread to the store shelves. Some products move very slowly. A few pharmaceutical drugs have supply chains that stretch out to more than 700 days. In the automotive industry, it may take months to convert different metals into the tubes, resonators, mufflers, hooks, and flanges that make up an exhaust system.

For products that are high value, time sensitive, security sensitive, or transformational in nature, there is a driving need to monitor and control the assets that are transporting them through their supply chains. For example, in the case of pharmaceutical drugs, counterfeit drugs represent 10% of the total supply in the worldwide marketplace and exceed 50% in some countries (the U.S. rate is said by the Food and Drug Administration to be much lower; we will discuss this in depth in Chapter 7).[9] The potential harmful exposure to humans and animals ingesting these drugs is very high. The U.S. Food and Drug Administration has issued its FDA Product Authentication guidelines that mandate chain-of-custody and other security measures to ensure products and their containers and transport vehicles are tamper-proof.[10] The U.S. Department of Defense with the U.S. Homeland Security Agency are working together to develop guidelines around the security of both armaments and food supplies. In all cases, the focus is on the security of the product and the security of the transport unit.

Monitoring of the Moving Asset— Value Proposition Expands

The monitoring of transport units has been around for approximately 25 years. For example, Cadec Global Inc. is a 30-year-old systems company that launched its first vehicle information system in 1981. This early version combined driver input with electronic Department of Transportation (DOT) log capability to produce an electronic driver trip report. By 1990, Cadec increased its functionality to compare the performance of the truck itself to actual truck performance standards. In 1992, Cadec developed SensorPLUS, a vehicle monitoring system that was integrated with Motorola's CoveragePLUS system, and Cadec/NORAND, an integrated system that uploaded vehicle, trip, and route accounting data.

In 1995, Cadec released RouteMessenger, a cellular technology-based driver communications and automatic transmission of trip information system. By 1998, Cadec added global positioning system (GPS) technology to allow for precise location tracking of trucks. In 2002, Cadec introduced TempTrackers, a system that wirelessly monitors and records the temperatures in trailers. In 2004, Cadec added a wireless sensor option for tracking trailer door events called DoorTracker.[11]

Cadec is focused on providing the complete trip information system for truck drivers and transport managers. The vehicle, trip, and route accounting data are wirelessly sent to the driver and manager primarily through a wireless local area network (WLAN).[12] What we like about Cadec is the fact that they are providing technology-based products to a specific supply chain industry segment that have defined value propositions.

Wireless Communications Networks

A wireless local area network is the linking of two or more computers or devices without using wires.[13] The de facto standard for these wireless connections is called Wi-Fi for the underlying technology for WLANs (Figure 2.1). A device such as a laptop, PDA, telephone, or Cadec unit can connect to the Internet when it comes in close proximity with an access point in the WLAN.[14] An access point is a hardware device with computer software that acts as a communications hub for users of a wireless device (such as a Cadec unit) to connect with a wired (or wireless) LAN.[15] The access point interacts with the sensors, stores the appropriate information, and sends the information when requested to the appropriate users through a WLAN connected to the users' systems.

In 1999, 3Com, Aironet/Cisco, Harris Semiconductor/Intersil, Lucent/Agere, Nokia, and Symbol Technologies formed the Wi-Fi Alliance. This alliance specifies methods and techniques (IEEE 802.11 standard) for WLAN operations, performs testing, and certifies interoperability of WLAN products. Security is still an issue, as well as the complexity of numerous versions of radio and data formats of the products. As such, interoperability is still a challenge despite the Wi-Fi Alliance and 802.11 specifications.[16]

Imagine a Cadec unit using Wi-Fi to connect to the user's enterprise systems through a WLAN. The process is similar to your laptop connecting through a wireless adapter and a wireless router to your cable or DSL connection to the Internet in your home. To secure your connection, you "program" your laptop with the router so that your router recognizes your laptop and "allows" the connection to occur. You also encrypt your connection to prevent easy theft of your wireless transmission. Encryption is the process of obscuring information to make it unreadable without special knowledge, using message authentication code or sometimes digital signatures.[17]

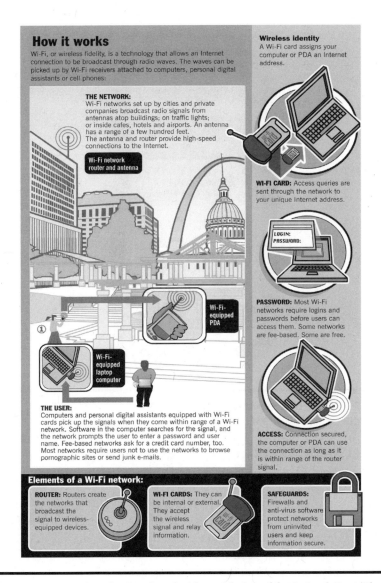

Figure 2.1   How W-Fi works. Reprinted with permission of the St. Louis Post-Dispatch, copyright 2009.

If a Cadec unit is using a "private" WLAN or is "registered" with the public WLAN, the access point will recognize the Cadec unit and allow an encrypted transfer of information to occur. However, if the unit is not registered and the WLAN is public, the transfer of information is open to piracy. This is the same situation as connecting your laptop in an Internet café or a Starbucks. Needless to say, caution needs to be exercised when confidential or proprietary information is being transmitted.

Figure 2.2   Sensitech TempTale.4 humidity sensor. Source: http://www.sensitech .com/products/hardware/temp_monitors/TT4_humidity.html.

SensiTech—Maximizing the Value of Transport Diagnostics

As Cadec focuses on a transport trip from a carrier perspective, another supply chain services company, Sensitech of Beverly, Massachusetts, focuses on deriving value for a shipper or consignee through post-trip analytic diagnostics. Sensitech is a Carrier Corporation division that specializes in cold chain visibility solutions in the food and pharmaceutical industries. Its products and services enable companies to track and monitor assets across the food and pharmaceutical supply chains. Their focus is on protecting the integrity of temperature-sensitive products through their trip-logging hardware and post-trip analytic services.[18] By understanding the "when and how" of temperature swings during a transport trip, the supply chain professional can take corrective action through process or technology modifications to their operating practices. Given the value of pharmaceutical drugs and selected food products, the knowledgeable corrective action taken by the supply chain professional can produce savings in the tens of millions of dollars for his or her company.

Cadec and Sensitech have both unlocked value in the supply chain for their customers using sensors and data-capturing devices in mobile assets. This benefit derived from the use of sensors is far beyond the capabilities of RFID technologies. It must be noted that Sensitech is an active member of EPCglobal Inc. and recognized as a leader in the move to automate the cold chain with radio frequency-enabled instruments and RFID technology. We believe Sensitech recognizes the short-term value of the use of sensors and the long-term potential value of RFID technology.

There is another level beyond the use of both sensors and RFID technology. Cadec and Sensitech primarily focus on products for trip logging and services for post-trip diagnostics. The next level or stage of value to be derived in the supply chain involves on-demand smart machine services *during* the transport of products.

Value Maximization in an On-Demand World

The transport of products involves mobile assets that include trucks, trains, airplanes, ocean vessels, barges, and personal vehicles such as vans, sport utility vehicles, and automobiles. Sometimes the movement of products takes hours, such as blood plasma products sent by airfreight to a medical facility or hospital. Other times, the movement of products can take days and even weeks, as in the case of fruit ripening en route to its destination. Whatever the mode of transport or the time, products are subject to environmental factors while they are in transport. These environmental factors range from vibration to atmosphere and temperature to humidity. Devices placed on the mobile assets can help monitor and control these environmental factors.

The communications to and from these devices is the critical success factor in taking supply chain automation to the next level of value. Mobile asset devices can connect through one of three ways. The first way to connect is to come into proximity of a WLAN using a Wi-Fi access point as we just discussed with Cadec and Sensitech. The second way to connect is through the use of satellite services (as Cadec can do); while the third way is to connect through the use of cellular communications.

The communications between a mobile asset device and an access point in a WLAN (and the transfer of trip data to the enterprise systems) rely on the mobile asset device coming into range of the Wi-Fi or "hot spot" connection. For products such as Cadec and Sensitech, this can be periodic throughout the trip or post-trip when the transport units return to a domicile. Although the value derived is a significant improvement over RFID, it is still "after the fact" when events occur on the road and out of the control of the responsible parties. Although corrective action can be taken, it is often hours, days, or sometimes weeks after the fact. Unfortunately, this does not help address the $1 million load of pharmaceutical drugs or the $125,000 load of prawns at risk when a refrigerated container unit (often called a reefer) fails.

When Time Is Money—The Satellite Option

Mobile asset devices can communicate to enterprise systems through the use of satellite broadband communications. For example, Qualcomm offers two services, OmniTRACS and OmniExpress, that help dedicated and for-hire transport companies track and control assets while they are en route to their destinations.

Satellite broadband communications help transport companies immensely when time-sensitive, security-sensitive, or high value loads are being transported. In addition, satellite communications are important when mobile assets are in rural or very remote areas where other means of communication are not available.

The cost of satellite broadband communications ranges from $1,250 per megabyte (MB) of data to more than $10,000/MB. If we assume a simple message has 70 bytes, then the minimum cost per message for satellite communications is $.068 per message.[19]

There are two basic types of satellite communications available for the movement of supply chain data. Geosynchronous satellites orbit the earth once every 24 hours at an altitude of approximately 36,000 kilometers. Because of its high orbit altitude, it has a "reach" that can transmit data within minutes (Figure 2.3). Low Earth orbit satellites orbit the Earth at altitudes of less than 2,000 kilometers. Their transmission times can range from 0 to 90 minutes, depending on the position of the satellite and its "reach" (Figure 2.4).[20]

Real supply chain costs can skyrocket when a catastrophic event (e.g., flood, theft, or failure of reefer unit) comes into play. An on-board device or access point that is accumulating event data can reach 1 MB of data in a matter of hours. Sending 4 to 6 hours of event data and spending $1,000 to $3,000 can be a lot of money for a

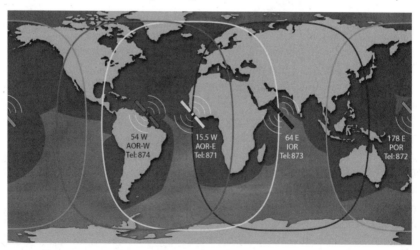

Figure 2.3 Geosynchronous satellite pathway. Source: Ray Hood and SensorLogic, adapted from InMarSat's Geo System Satellite Coverage Map.

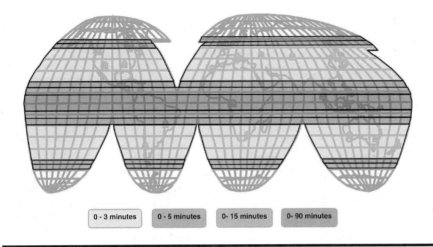

| 0 - 3 minutes | 0 - 5 minutes | 0- 15 minutes | 0- 90 minutes |

Figure 2.4 Satellite transmission times for low Earth orbits. Source: Ray Hood and SensorLogic.

$3,000 load of potatoes. However, it is a small amount of money when considering our previous example of pharmaceuticals or prawns. Furthermore, it could be priceless when armaments or food supplies are being tampered with by terrorists.

When Time Is Money—And Money Matters: The Cellular Option

Devices in mobile assets (as well as devices on fixed assets where wirelines are not accessible) can communicate through a wireless wide area network (WWAN). Unlike a WLAN, a wireless wide area network uses cellular technologies to transfer data. These cellular technologies that transfer data are provided by the same wireless carriers that provide voice services on a subscription basis, including but not limited to Cingular, Sprint PCS, T-Mobile, Vodafone, Verizon, and many others.

Many computer-based devices on assets now have integrated WWAN capabilities. They have these capabilities through the insertion of a cellular radio into the device with GSM (the world standard) or CDMA (pioneered by Qualcomm and used widely in the United States, China, and some other countries) connections, which allow the user of the device to send and receive data.[21]

There are numerous technologies involved in an integrated WWAN. The following are the top three technologies that affect the business application of moving data in the supply chain.

GSM is the global system for mobile communications. This system, used by more than 3 billion people around the world, allows for international roaming between mobile phone operators. The system is designed around digital call quality, which means it is a 2G (second-generation) mobile phone system and has the ability for data communication in addition to voice communication. Subscribers can use their phones or devices in many parts of the world and have voice or data service through these roaming agreements.[22]

GPRS stands for general packet radio service. GPRS is a mobile data service available to users of GSM mobile phones. GPRS, when combined with 2G cellular systems, is frequently defined as 2.5G with moderate speed data transfer.[23]

CDMA2000 (code division multiple access) is a form of multiplexing and a method of multiple accesses that does not divide up the communications channel by time or frequency. Instead, data is encoded with a special code associated with each channel. CDMA is used in many communications systems, including in GPS and Qualcomm's OmniTRACS satellite system we cited earlier for transportation logistics. CDMA is also the basis for cellular voice services from providers like Sprint.[24]

GSM and CDMA both have their advantages, depending on the business or personal users and their needs. CDMA, created by Qualcomm, was the dominant network standard in North America and made significant inroads in Asia. GSM, the dominant network standard in Europe, has now become the leading voice network in the rest of the world as well.[25]

For the supply chain professional focused on the transfer of data, the CDMA2000 data transfer rate is between 300 and 700 kilobits (kb) per second, while GSM's data transfer rate is estimated at 384 kb. Even though GSM has a slower data transfer rate, it uses subscriber identity module (SIM) cards that allow devices (or phones) to be recognized by a cellular GSM carrier. Upgrading the device involves upgrading the SIM card. CDMA, on the other hand, uses a removable user identity module, or R-UIM, card that is placed in a proprietary device and is linked to one cellular network carrier. The new device must be upgraded, with the old one discarded. GSM is far superior in roaming with other GSM carriers.[26]

For the supply chain professional, money does matter. The use of cellular communications is far cheaper than the use of satellite broadband communications. For example, the same message (70 bytes) sent to or from a device on a mobile asset using a GSM/GPRS cellular carrier costs approximately 1/100th of the cost of satellite communications. The three- to five-year outlook for cellular data transmission costs is even more favorable for commercial use versus satellite broadband communications costs as advanced 3G networks are rolled out that combine some of the best features of GSM (global standards) and CDMA (better speed). The most important thing to remember as a supply chain professional is that the communications costs of your application will, over the lifetime of its deployment, likely be the largest cost—greater than hardware, software, or implementation services.

Although the cost of cellular communications is dramatically lower, the complexity is much higher. Service coverage and roaming agreements make consistent communications a challenge. In addition, the myriad of billing issues regarding each carrier and the associated taxation regulations combine to present a daunting challenge to even the most sophisticated commercial user of communications services.

Sensor Success Stories—Almost!

Fred spent a half-day with a leading truck insurance company discussing the use of sensors in the supply chain. An insurance company was selected because of the value proposition to shippers and carriers regarding the preservation of cargo. Many trucking companies are self-insured up to a certain amount of money. Insurance companies frequently get involved when the frequency of claims or the total dollar amount of claims exceeds certain agreed-to threshold limits. This insurance company agreed to speak with Fred on one condition—names, places, and dates were not to be used in the book. The following examples represent a summary of Fred's discussion.

One leading truck insurance company interviewed for this book had a great—and true—story to tell regarding the use of sensors. This truck insurance company insures the transport of high value commodities that need refrigerated service. These commodities include items such as meat, seafood, and certain pharmaceutical drugs.

Their journey with "the bad guys" started a few years ago. They recommended that their insured carriers install door open-and-close sensors with logging devices to detect when and where the doors were opened. The use of these door open-and-close sensors would allow the carriers to compare the information from the logging device with the driver's electronic trip logs. This comparison would determine the valid—and invalid—openings of the trailer doors. The carrier could determine when and where the invalid door openings occurred.

The door open-and-close sensors worked for a while, and lost or stolen claims decreased. It did not take long before lost or stolen merchandise claims increased to their pre-door open-and-close sensor levels. The insurance company had a few agents follow selected trucks on high-theft routes to determine how the thefts were carried out. These agents would use the trip manifests to identify the high-theft lanes, cross-reference them with the load manifests for the trailer completed by the shipper using RFID at the loading dock, and determine what trailers were "high risk." These "high-risk" trailers were the ones selected by the agents to follow on their routes.

At a popular truck stop in the southwest, one of the trucks being followed pulled up and entered one of the maintenance bays at 2:00 a.m. Using cameras with high-powered lenses, the agents watched in amazement as the maintenance worker carefully—and rapidly—pulled off the whole door without disturbing the door open-and-close sensor. Merchandise was quickly trans-loaded to a nearby truck, and the door was carefully replaced without disturbing the door open-and-close sensor. In this specific case, the insurance company was quick to point out that the driver never knew that the theft occurred!

The insurance company took quick action to place sensors on the door hinges as well. This action helped again for a short period of time. However, the thefts returned to the old levels.

The insurance company dispatched more agents to follow selected trucks on high-theft lanes. Once again, it did not take long for the agents to discover how theft was occurring and bypassing the door sensors.

The agents followed a handful of trucks until the driver stopped at a motel for a 10-hour rest. While the driver was in the motel sleeping, the bad guys drove up to the truck in a panel truck with "truck reefer maintenance" on the side. They proceeded to remove the entire refrigerated unit, climb inside the truck trailer, and remove merchandise through the hole left by removing the refrigerated unit. In one case, boxed beef was removed from the truck trailer. In another case, frozen shrimp was removed. The bad guys would replace the refrigerated unit after the theft and leave. The driver never knew that the theft occurred.

In this last case, most refrigerated units are now riveted to the truck trailers versus being bolted to the truck trailers, with sensors placed on the units themselves. This has stopped much of the theft through removing the refrigerated units, but has not stopped the practice altogether. Some bad guys rip the units out, while others carefully cut the rivets out and trying to re-rivet the units back into the truck trailer.

This journey did not surprise the insurance company, because they knew the bad guys were smart. (It did surprise Fred, that is for sure!) However, the insurance company continues on and is excited about the prospect of remote monitoring these units in a real-time manner. They also know that there is a significant need to "layer" security sensors to make it more difficult for thieves to penetrate truck trailers with high value loads. (We bet the agents who are asked to follow these trucks at 2:00 a.m. are happy to see remote monitoring employed by these carriers as well!)

Sometimes the Bad Guys Are Smart but Unlucky

Recently the insurance company started paying theft and damage claims to a tucking company that specializes in transporting meat products at subzero temperatures. The bad guys would cut a hole in the roof of the reefer and, using a jack, would pull up the beef through the hole and out of the refrigerated trailer. The bad guys would weld a patch on the hole and re-seal the trailer. The refrigerated unit and the door open-and-close sensors were not disturbed.

Traditionally, refrigerated trailer manufactures used fiberglass and plywood to insulate a trailer. This method proved to be adequate for refrigerated products and lightly frozen products (26° to 32° Fahrenheit). This method did not do well for products such as ice cream, meat products, and selected pharmaceutical drugs requiring subzero environments.

Some trailer manufacturers improved their processes and started spraying foam versus using fiberglass to insulate the trailers. This process improved the quality of the insulation, but was not a perfect solution. Trailer manufacturing workers would have to shave the spray foam to fit the plywood over it and maintain the minimum inside dimensions of the trailer. (This is extremely important for maximizing the cubic feet or weight of the payloads on the trailer.)

Some trailer manufacturers such as Great Dane have advanced the foam process and now use a foam press method for the foam insulation. This helps avoid the need to cut the foam to fit the plywood over it, thus compromising the integrity of the foam. Some of these trailers have insulated roof panels in addition to wall and floor panels. Some other trailers have plain non-insulated aluminum roofs on the trailers.

The bad guys would do their best to select the trailers with the non-insulated aluminum roofs. They were particularly skilled at "patching" aluminum trailers when the trailer skins were damaged. They by-passed the door open-and-close sensors and avoided "ripping out" the reefer unit to get into the trailer. They were smart—but unlucky.

The trucking company set up a truck-rail-truck door-to-door service, frequently called "piggyback" or trailer-on-flatcar. The trucking company set up its drivers to pick up the refrigerated loads from the shippers and take the loads to the railroad's intermodal yards. The railroad would transport these refrigerated trailers to another intermodal yard in another city. The trucking company would have its destination drivers pick up the refrigerated trailer from the destination intermodal facility and deliver the load to the consignee. The trucking company set up this operation for two reasons. The first reason is cost. The point-to-point linehaul cost on the railroad is much less than the linehaul cost for the trucking company. When the tonnage balance is accounted for, the linehaul costs go up because of the lack of available backhaul loads. The second reason is the quality of life for the drivers. Drivers are in short supply. By keeping drivers within a day's drive between shipment pick-up or delivery points and the rail intermodal yards (~450 miles), they can get their drivers home at a minimum of every other night. For many truckload operations, the drivers can spend up to three weeks on the road before they get home for a few days. It does not take a mathematician to figure out which is better from a quality of life standpoint.

Because the bad guys picked refrigerated trailers that were used in a piggyback operation, they were outfitted with specialized vibration sensors similar to ones used on railcars. When the bad guys cut into the roofs of the trailers, they bypassed the door open-and-close sensors and the refrigerated units themselves. However, they set off the vibration sensors. Once again, the insurance agents were able to compare the driver trip logs with the vibration sensor activity to pinpoint the times and places where the thefts occurred. These agents set up a sting operation and were able to catch the bad guys. Sometimes it is better to be lucky than be good—just ask the bad guys!

Insurance Company Summary

The insurance company is an integral part of the transport industry and the overall supply chain. They were very knowledgeable of sensors and their application to protect high value cargo from both environmental conditions and "the bad guys." They also work hard to help train the internal security and internal over short and damage (OS&D) department of the trucking firms they insure.

The insurance company is also excited about the ability to remotely monitor and control trailers and containers. We will cover remote monitoring and control of transport units in Chapter 5 and other chapters. They were also very knowledgeable about the use of multilayering sensors to increase the effectiveness of the use of sensors. They believe—as we do—that multilayering also increases the level of complexity for the bad guys, creating a deterrent for many of them. We will discuss multilayering for load and cargo protection in Chapter 7 when we review the role of Authentix in the pharmaceutical industry.

This insurance company also believes that RFID technology helps identify what cargo is placed on what trailer. However, it believes that sensor technologies offer a different yet complementary dimension of cargo protection. It has shown to us that the bad guys are smart, sophisticated, and determined to steal their targeted cargo. For shippers and carriers waiting for RFID technology to mature and not making the effort to explore other technologies (e.g., sensors), they are allowing the bad guys to get the upper hand. As the insurance company told Fred, both the carriers and shippers can invest in alternative technologies to deter the bad guys, or they can let the bad guys win and pay for it in obscene insurance rates. They can pay now or pay more later!

Summary

The use of sensors in the supply chain is not new. It does, however, take the effectiveness of the RFID world to another level. In addition, the use of access points with embedded software makes it possible to remotely monitor and control both fixed and mobile assets. The business value associated with addressing supply chain issues in near real-time increases as the security, value, and/or time sensitivity of the products being shipped increases. The cost/benefit analysis of remotely monitoring and control assets must take the cost of communications into account when doing the analysis.

Notes

1. Answers.com, Sensor. http://www.answers.com/topic/sensor?cat=technology.
2. http://en.wikipedia.org/wiki/Sensor; and Kliff Black.
3. Ibid.
4. Austin R. Mills, Lead Developer, SensorLogic, October 3, 2006.
5. http://inventors.about.com/library/inventors/blseismograph11.htm; and http://www.bookrags.com/research.seismograph-woes-02/.

6. Dr. Kliff Black, SensorLogic, September 21, 2006.
7. http://en.wikipedia.org/wiki/Landline.
8. Fred A. Kuglin, personal experience and projects with food manufacturers.
9. U.S. Food and Drug Administration, "Counterfeit Drugs Questions and Answers." http://www.fda.gov/oc/initiatives/counterfeit/qa.html.
10. Code of Federal Regulations, CFR Title 21 Part 203. http://www.fda.gov/OHRMS/DOCKETS/98fr/06-5362.htm.
11. http://www.cadec.com/about_us/history.htm.
12. Ibid.
13. http://en.wikipedia.org/wiki/Wi-Fi.
14. Ibid.
15. http://www.webopedia.com/TERM/A/AP.html; and Ray Hood.
16. http://en.wikipedia.org/wiki/Wi-Fi; and Kliff Black.
17. http://en.wikipedia.org/wiki/Encryption and http://en.wikipedia.org/wiki/Wi-Fi_Alliance; and Fred Kuglin.
18. http://www.sensitech.com/; and Peter Maysek, VP Marketing SensiTech (approved marked-up Word document sent to Fred A. Kuglin April 18, 2008 for use in book).
19. Dr. Kliff Black, September 21, 2006.
20. http://www.geo-orbit.org/sizepgs/geodef.html; and Kliff Black.
21. http://en.wikipedia.org/wiki/WWAN; and Kliff Black.
22. http://en.wikipedia.org/wiki/Gsm; and Fred Kuglin.
23. http://en.wikipedia.org/wiki/Gprs.
24. http://www.wisegeek.com/what-is-the-difference-between-gsm-and-cdma.htm; and Fred Kuglin and Ray Hood.
25. Ibid.
26. Ibid.

Chapter 3

Tracking Animals and Other Living Beings: From Farm to Fork and from Home to School (Hopefully!)

Agriculture, manufactures, commerce, and navigation, the four pillars of our prosperity, are then most thriving when left most free to individual enterprise.

Thomas Jefferson

Farming looks mighty easy when your plow is a pencil, and you're a thousand miles from the corn field.

Dwight D. Eisenhower

As a parent, you think you have control of your children—until they begin to drive!

Anonymous

Introduction

The use of radio frequency identification (RFID) and sensor technologies to track animals, marine life, and people has dramatically increased in the mid-2000s. The tracking of animals from farm to fork is extremely valuable to increase efficiency and ensure the safety of our food supply chain. The tracking of marine life helps researchers understand the ecology of the marine life and encourage others to protect our marine food supply. The tracking of pets helps protect the owners from a devastating loss when the pet gets away from their control. The tracking of people (from teenagers to criminals) has their own value propositions to parents and society in general.

In this chapter, we will review the tracking of animals (specifically hogs) and their environment from farm to fork. We will review how the use of the same technologies extends beyond the supply chain to track marine life, pets, and people.

Food Supply Chain: Pork

The food supply chain provides supply to meet a constantly renewed demand. People eat multiple times a day, generating this demand. (This is opposed to a DVD supply chain, which provides supply to meet a one-time demand.) There are many people who will argue that demand comes first, while others argue that supply comes first to generate the demand. This sounds like the proverbial question, "Which came first, the chicken or the egg?" To further complicate matters, the compression of time between demand and supply has been so great in the last several years that the answer is really convoluted.

Let us take for instance the Jimmy Dean sausage commercial about the sun and breakfast. The sausage in the commercial being consumed and promoted by "the sun" represents supply, while the desire of "the sun" to eat the sausage is the demand. "The sun" is actually the end of the supply chain. The Sara Lee Corporation, owners of the Jimmy Dean brand of sausage, is the final supplier, and represents "supply." The commercial is fun to watch, and its message ("The Day Begins With a Happy Breakfast") is designed to generate demand for the sausage. The pork supply chain, focused on providing supply to meet the demand, has several value-added steps that begin with a live animal raised for the specific purpose of becoming sausage and other pork products.

The pork supply chain and hog farming overall have become a very lucrative, complex, and in many respects a scientific supply chain process. We have come a long way from a dozen pigs in a pen (and one boar of course). We will for this chapter start with reviewing the size of the industry and how supply is produced, or more appropriately "raised."

Worldwide, 97,200,000 metric tons of pork are estimated to have been produced in 2006. The United States represents 10,070,000 metric tons, or 10.36%, of the worldwide total production. The world's largest producers of pork are China at an estimated 52,000,000 metric tons and the EU-25 at 21,500,000 metric tons. Taken as an aggregate, the size of the hog industry worldwide is significant.[1] Let's look at the individual components that make up the hog supply chain.

From Birth to Processing Plant

The process starts with an "integrator." An integrator is the source of the "genetics" (young pigs with a known genotype). Integrators track the lineage of millions of pigs and can predict, based on the linage, the "yield weight" and even the "slaughter date" based on a set number of assumptions around feed, temperature, and other growing factors.

The integrator facilitates the impregnation of the sows. The sows will give birth to piglets in a farrowing facility. A normal litter is 6 to 12 piglets. These piglets are raised for 20 days in the farrowing facility. At the ripe age of 20 days, these piglets are taken to a growing house called a "nursery." These nurseries are owned by "growers," who contract with integrators to raise the piglets (sometimes they are direct employees of the integrators). The growers will do one of two things: either (a) raise the 20-day-old piglets to approximately 50 pounds and then send them to a finishing house, or (b) they will raise the 20-day-old piglets straight through finishing to their slaughter or "processing" size. The latter nurseries are called "wean to finish" farms.

The optimal "processing weight" for a hog is 180 pounds. However, hogs can often grow to 240 to 300 pounds or more. Given the variety of the pork products sold in grocery stores, any weight more than 180 pounds tends to produce more fat and waste and less meat yield on a ratio to total weight basis. Note that the total calendar time from birth to "processing" or slaughter is approximately 180 days—a weight gain of 1 pound every day! After reaching a target weight, hogs are loaded as a batch (or sub-batch) onto a truck to go to a processing plant. (The processing plant to store-shelf part of "farm to fork" will be covered later.)

In the end, like any business, it is all about money. Let us take a look at a pro forma P&L for growing hogs (Table 3.1).

The largest cost categories are the feeder pigs themselves, the feed for the pigs, and the capital costs to outfit the farrowing facilities and grow houses. There is an intense need to manage the cost components in each one of these cost categories for the integrators to maintain their overall margins in producing pork products.

Technology has affected the "farm-to-processing plant" portion of the farm-to-fork supply chain in a major way. The primary measurement for integrators and growers in the farm-to-processing plant portion of the supply chain is the "feed-to-meat" ratio, more commonly referred to in the industry as the "feed-grain" ratio. Integrators provide the feed and medicine, while the growers supply the barns, electricity, water, fuel, and labor.

Table 3.1 Hog Production Costs and Returns per Hundredweight (cwt) Gain, 2004–2005. Source: http://ers.usda.gov/Data/CostsAndReturns/testpick.htm, "Hogs-All."

	United States	
	2004	*2005*
Item	*$/cwt gain*	*$/cwt gain*
Gross value of production		
Market hogs	50.17	51.18
Feeder pigs	13.97	17.37
Cull stock	0.73	0.74
Breeding stock	0.06	0.06
Inventory change	−0.87	0.34
Other income	1.74	2.04
Total, gross value of production	65.80	71.73
Operating costs		
Feed		
Grain	2.99	2.32
Protein sources	2.61	1.96
Complete mixes	16.18	14.16
Other feed items	0.12	0.1
Total feed cost	21.90	18.54
Other		
Feeder pigs	17.98	22.52
Veterinary and medicine	0.88	0.90
Bedding and litter	0.02	0.02
Marketing	0.78	0.81
Custom services	0.28	0.28
Fuel, lube, and electricity	0.96	1.32

Table 3.1 (continued)   Hog Production Costs and Returns per Hundredweight (cwt) Gain, 2004–2005

	United States	
	2004	*2005*
Item	*$/cwt gain*	*$/cwt gain*
Other (continued)		
Repairs	0.69	0.72
Interest on operating capital	0.34	0.76
Total, operating costs	43.83	45.87
Allocated overhead		
Hired labor	1.66	1.68
Opportunity cost of unpaid labor	3.58	3.51
Capital recovery of machinery and equipment	6.68	7.05
Opportunity cost of land (rental rate)	0.03	0.03
Taxes and insurance	0.57	0.58
General farm overhead	1.42	1.49
Total, allocated overhead	13.94	14.34
Total costs listed	57.77	60.21
Value of production less total costs listed	8.03	11.52
Value of production less operating costs	21.97	25.86
Supporting information		
Production arrangement (percent of production)		
Independent	41	40
Under contract	59	60
Size of operation (head sold/removed)		
Market hogs	2,669	2,761
Feeder pigs	2,437	2,515

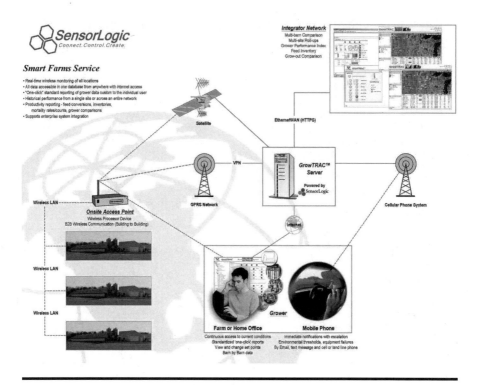

Figure 3.1   The Sensorlogic Smart Farms Services model. Source: Sensorlogic, Inc.

A Dallas-based technology firm, Sensorlogic, has developed its Smart Farms Service leveraging sensors and wireless communications to help integrators and growers improve the feed-to-meat ratios in the farm-to-processing plant supply chain (see Exhibit B). In grower facilities (barns), electronic controllers operating through sensors and actuators control heaters, fans, cooling devices, feeders, water meters, lights, and other equipment used to determine the exact environmental conditions for the hogs. These electronic controllers are used to keep environmental factors within defined ranges to maximize the comfort (and thus the eventual weight) of the pig. Sensorlogic's Smart Farms Service lets these business rules be automatically enforced so that integrators and growers can remotely monitor and control their barn operations. It is all about maximizing yield while minimizing cost.

In the Sensorlogic model, data is transmitted (via landline, cellular, or satellite) from the grower barns to a software service maintained on the Internet so that both the growers and the integrators can access the information. Once the data is flowing, the integrator can monitor grower performance, barn-specific performance, multibarn comparisons, grow-out comparisons, and overall "alarms." These alarms can range from high-energy costs to equipment failures to environmental thresholds. In addition, low fuel tanks or low feed levels can be monitored. This way, various operations around the country can be compared and best practices can be refined.

"Supply" in the supply chain is also all about "yield." Low fuel tank alarms can alert the proper people to avoid a fuel outage, as well as loss of animals. Responding to low feed level alarms can prevent the outage of feed, as well as the negative impact on supply and yield. In addition, the data can be processed to perform predictive diagnostics. For example, hogs overeat when they are stressed. This stress can come from temperature issues or disease such as swine flu. Early detection of temperature problems will prevent underweight hogs (the eventual result of overeating followed by undereating) or delays in processing dates—both of which represent costs to integrators and growers as well as the processing plant companies. The early detection of disease can prevent the loss of large numbers of hogs—a substantial loss of investment to integrators and growers and a loss of supply to processing plant companies. Both issues contribute to disruptions in distribution channels when alternative supply sources are introduced for the processing plants. In severe cases, these issues contribute to a loss of meat products on store shelves, resulting in lost market share for retailers, processing plant companies, distributors, and eventually the integrators and growers. In severe cases, everyone in the supply chain loses.

The impact of the loss in the supply chain is directly proportional to the share of the retail pork value in the supply chain. For $100 of pork products sold by the retailer, $31.10 goes to the grower; $13.10 goes to the integrator; and $55.80 goes to the processor, the final wholesale distributor (if one is involved), and the retailer.[2] Although both the integrators and the growers are concerned with the survivability of the pigs and the overall yield of the hogs, there are differences. Growers look to technology to help them monitor and control the growing process from a remote location. Integrators are interested in utilizing technology to maximize the performance of various growers across a broad spectrum. They are both battling to maximize their share of the store-door value of the delivered pork products.

From Processing Plant to Store Shelf

The integrators are responsible for the reacquisition of mature hogs from the farmers and delivering them to the processing plants. In many instances, these integrators own the processing plants and coordinate the delivery of the pork products to the ultimate retailers.

It was identified in Exhibit A that 60% of hogs are grown under contract. From the integrator or processor's perspective, the contracted hog percentage is frequently augmented by participation in hog futures. When added together, integrators or processors lock into the committed supply for their processing plants, up to 90% of a total production capacity.

It was mentioned earlier that hogs can grow from an optimal weight of 180 pounds to a total of 240 to 300 pounds. The integrator prefers the optimal weight of 180 pounds because of the higher prices that retailers pay for lean, boneless loins and hams. In addition, approximately 72% to 74% of the hog is used for meat, with other parts (e.g., bones, blood, etc.) contributing to revenue-producing purposes.

Despite the optimal weight of 180 pounds preferred by the integrators, the growers prefer the heaviest hogs possible because they are frequently compensated on a gross per pound basis. The use of technology by integrators to monitor grower performance in hog feed and hog weight is increasingly being used to maximize the return on investment for the integrators—and manage the "push/pull" between growers and integrators on the best processing weight for the hogs.

Integrators and processors are using RFID and sensor technologies to track and monitor hogs from farms to processing plants, from processing plants to finishing or tray-packing plants, and from tray-packing plants to retail distribution stores or to retail distribution centers. In the future, wireless sensors will be used to monitor and control the conditions of the transport and cooler or refrigerator units. (More on this in the cold chain section in Chapter 5.)

The speed of the movement (or throughput) of the hogs from the processing plant to store shelf is critical to all involved. Frequently, the supply (and store-door price) of pork at the retail store is controlled by a "category captain" or a "category manager." This individual usually works for a company that has a large market share in the overall "category" in the store. The responsibility of the category manager is to set the category "plan-o-grams" based on supplier performance in market share, volumes, pricing, and sales per square foot for each product. Macro- and micro-economic forces, along with seasonal, geographic, and weather-related conditions, are inputs into the category manager's system to produce an optimal mix of products at target prices.

The supply chain must be able to respond within 24 to 48 hours to match supply with demand. The category manager will "reset" stores and recommend daily pricing with regional retail managers to optimize category performance on a day-to-day basis. The movement of supply to accommodate these last minute decisions must be based on supply chain professionals knowing where the supply of pork is at any given point in time. This also includes the condition of the pork and its environment and the code dates of the tray-packed product.

Cost of Supply Disruptions

Large integrators such as Cargill, Inc. and Smithfield, Inc. have hundreds of processing plants throughout North America and numerous processing plants around the world. Because of the perishability of pork products, the value per pound of pork produced, and environmental regulations, the large integrators locate processing plants in primarily rural areas in reasonably close proximity to major population (or consumption) centers.

Typically these processing plants have assigned customers to provide pork products. Customers such as Wal-Mart demand next day replenishment of stock or everyday items such as pork chops or hams. There exists only a day or two of inventory of many pork products.

Disruptions in supply can have huge cost impacts to integrators. If a disease breaks out and causes a number of hogs to be destroyed, the integrators must search for replacements as quickly as possible. The total remaining supply of hogs, coupled with the production from each processing plant and the demand from the top customers, must be reviewed to determine the strategy to protect the required product deliveries for the top customers.

The results from a supply disruption range from minimal to devastating. If the loss of supply is small, there may be no loss in terms of providing pork products to grocery stores. The impact is lost (and lower margin) product sales to alternative distribution channels (food service, restaurants, etc.) that normally provide an outlet for the excess supply of pork products. If there is a moderate loss of supply, the integrator may be forced to use pork products from more remote processing plants and send these pork products greater distances to meet the demand. The increased costs may range from overtime labor in the processing plants to greater trucking costs. If there is a significant loss in supply, the integrator may be forced to buy supply from its competitors, run overtime in its plants, incur greater trucking costs, and, in extreme instances, short the store shelves of pork products.

It is imperative that integrators adopt the best technology capable of predicting disruptions in supply (disease, etc.) to avoid the range of bad-to-worse cost implications that result from supply disruptions.[3]

Tracking Devices: Not New with Animal and Marine Life Tracking

The tracking of animals (and humans for that matter) is not new. One company, Sonotronics, is a leader in the design and manufacture of ultrasonic tracking systems. It has been in business since 1971, and has pioneered the development of coded sonic transmitters for tracking marine animals such as whales, sharks, turtles, and trout. Sonotronics's tracking systems also have been used in marking submerged underwater equipment for later relocation to other sites.

Sonotronics uses transmitters that range from accelerometers to temperature, depth, and location markers that work with surface, subsurface, or diver receivers. Trackers use directional or omnidirectional hydrophones to locate subsurface transmitters.[4]

In 2003, thanks to funding from conservation groups and the South African government, 25 great white sharks were tagged with satellite tracking devices off the coast of South Africa. The majority of the great white sharks maintained coastal migration along the South African coastline. One great white shark was tracked on a 12,000-mile journey from South Africa to Australia and back. This female great white shark, nicknamed "Nicole" after the Australian actress Nicole

Figure 3.2a   Dr. Ramón Bonfil with the PAT Tag. Source: http://www.shark-tracker.com/en/Tagging/Pop-up-archival-tags/index.php.

Kidman, provided the first proof that the shark populations of these two Southern Hemisphere continents were in fact linked.[5] Dr. Ramón Bonfil, who participated in the tagging and tracking of "Nicole," is pictured with the popup archival tag (PAT Tag) used to track "Nicole" in Figure 3.2a. Figure 3.2b is a great white shark with the PAT tag.

For the researchers, the monitoring of migration patterns of great white sharks provided significant discoveries for shark ecology and conservation purposes. For the purpose of our book, the tracking of a shark long distances with a sensor-based tracking device provides significant learning for the tracking of ranging animals such as cattle.

From Sharks to Cows and Other Farm Animals

TekVet, an agricultural technology company, has developed a monitoring technology for livestock. This monitoring technology allows cattle producers to monitor location and core body temperature data of individual cattle in real-time through the Internet. Monitoring the body temperature of individual cattle can help cattle producers identify and inoculate sick cattle, preventing the loss of the one head as

Figure 3.2b A great white shark with the PAT Tag. Source: Michael School. http://www.shark-tracker.com/en/Tagging/Pop-up-archival-tags/index.php.

Figure 3.3 The TekVet TekSensor. Source: http://www.tekvet.com/.

well as the spreading of infectious diseases to other cattle in the herd by segregating infected animals from the herd.[6]

TekVet uses the TekSensor, an active RFID tag that is attached to the cow's ear (Figure 3.3). The TekSensor includes a flexible thermometer and a wireless transceiver. The transmitting range for the TekSensor is 500–1500 feet. Location and body temperature data is transmitted to wireless receiving stations on a cattle producer's lot as the cows come into range. The data is then transported by a private satellite network to TekVet's central network operations center. The data is compiled and made available to producers and regulatory agencies via the Internet. Included in the reports are the identification of abnormalities, trend analysis, and historical archiving.[7]

The historical archiving is critical to the tracking of beef from "farm to fork." Currently the TekVet solution exceeds the USDA standards, and meets many of the FDA tracking requirements under consideration and rollout at press time of this book.

Sharks and cows are both mobile and have significant ranging distances. This is why both examples (sharks and cows) rely on the use of satellite tracking. For sharks, a sensor-based device is used. For cows, an active RFID tag or sensor is used. In both cases, data on the animals is transmitted to interpret the ecology and health of the animals. In addition, both examples have advanced the cause to track food supply from "farm to fork" and help ensured the safety of our food supply.

The excitement for the use of RFID technology is very high in the food supply chain. According to the study, "RFID for Animals, Food and Farming 2007–2017" by Dr. Peter Harrop, Ning Xiao, and Glyn Holland, the global spending for RFID systems and tags is expected to increase to $5.8 billion in 2017.[8] This includes the tagging of individual items, pallets, cases, vehicles, and equipment. (We are still waiting for the first billion to materialize, but progress is occurring in several applications.)

Ancillary Benefits

Occasionally, deep-sea divers get lost subsurface. When this happens, time is of the essence due to limited oxygen supplies and other subsurface threats and hazards. The same technology used in transmitters attached to whales and sharks is used in deep-sea tracking devices known as "pingers." (Sonotronics has a driver tracking system available and tested for such an application.) Deep-sea diving clubs or government regulatory agencies dictate the transmitting (beacon operating) frequency used by the pingers and deep-sea divers. The topside receivers or "echosounders" must match the transmitting frequency of the pingers to pick up the signals. Different sizes and uses of vessels operating in different depths of water command different echosounders. Divers in the 0 to 60 meter range can have their pingers picked up by a robust fish finder. Divers who go into waters 100 to 130 meters deep need a fairly sophisticated echosounder.[9]

The trouble occurs when divers go missing and other vessels are called in to help locate the divers. Time is of the essence, and valuable time could be lost searching for the right vessel with a suitable echosounder. It is important to make sure that the transmitting frequency and the echosounder on the host vessel match before divers enter the water. (To nondivers, standardization across the board appears to be needed to avoid the endless "version control" issues and late adoption of life-saving technology that are available today.)

Divers are not on top of the food chain when they are subsurface. It is important to adopt the right technology as an industry to prevent the divers from being part—the wrong part—of the food supply chain.

Tracking in the Pork Supply Chain

The United States Department of Agriculture (USDA) is sponsoring the National Animal Identification System (NAIS) effort. The Pork Industry Identification Working Group has taken the lead to recommend how their industry would like to proceed with the implementation of a national swine ID system. On July 22, 2006, the Pork Industry Identification Working Group submitted its recommendations to the NAIS Subcommittee of the Secretary's Advisory Committee of Foreign Animal and Poultry Diseases of the USDA. The goal of their recommendations is to enable animal health officials to perform a systematic trace-back within 48 hours of the discovery of a catastrophic swine disease.[10]

Two key components of the NAIS are animal identification and animal tracing. Animal identification involves an animal identification number (AIN) that is unique and stays with the animal for its lifetime. This number links the animal to its birthplace or premises of origin. Currently this program is voluntary. There are two options: individual identification and group or lot identification. The group or lot identification is for animals that "stay together" as one group throughout their lifetimes, such as hogs.[11]

Animal tracing allows for the tracking of the animals as they travel through the supply chain. Private or state databases will maintain this tracking information, and will only be requested or disclosed if a disease or health event occurs. We

Figure 3.4   A Cargill pork lot. Cargill, Pork, Products & Services. Source: http://www.cargillanimalnutrition.com/pork/dc_can_pork.htm.

believe that access to this information will allow health officials to isolate the health or disease outbreak and contain the collateral damage from an infected animal.

The Pork Industry Identification Working Group made several recommendations that impressed the authors. The first recommendation is to standardize the swine identification methods. This is absolutely essential for obvious reasons. Another recommendation is to leave open-ended the technologies that will enable animal tracking. They recommend "Given the present uncertainties associated with implementing a fully operational real-time animal health ID tracking system across all species under a voluntary 'technology neutral' system." In other words, they will support whatever technology works today to enable animal tracking.[12]

Tracking Pets

In the United States alone, a family pet is lost *every two seconds!* More than six to eight million cats and dogs enter shelters every year. Their owners eventually reclaim only 600,000 to 750,000 from shelters, or roughly 10% of the total.[13]

Some of these "lost pets" are in reality abandoned by their owners. The vast majority of these dogs and cats are pets that get out of the house without leashes and get lost. For the owners, the loss of a pet can be a devastating experience. Using the same base technologies that monitor the environment for hogs and track ranging cows, a few enterprising companies have launched pet tracking services using pet tracker collars.

Micro Tech (now AirtightVideo.com) has developed a pet tracker collar that works for a week on the internal re-chargeable battery. The collar fastens to the pet's existing collar. The collar device can operate in two modes: Standard/Walk and Geofence. In Standard mode, if the pet gets away, the owner can get notifications on the Web site, phone, or via a pet locator specialist. In Geofence mode, the owner specifies the containment area radius, and if the pet wanders from that containment area, the owner will be notified.[14]

Globalpetfinder has a product designed for dogs 11 pounds and heavier (Figure 3.5). Owners build a geofence with the help of Globalpetfinder. If the pet wanders outside of the geofence, alerts are sent with the exact location of the pet. This product weighs 5 ounces, uses rechargeable batteries, and can connect to a cell phone, PDA, laptop, or any other communications device.[15]

The Pointer Dog-GPS is manufactured by Pointer Positioning Solutions. One device is placed on the dog's collar, while the hunter has a map device with GPS. The hunter can watch the dog's position on the map device screen. The Pointer Dog-GPS product has audio capabilities as well, so the hunter can listen to what is going on at the dog's location.[16]

Of course, there are downsides to tracking pets that have the misfortune to wander away from home. In many states, the threat of coyotes and bobcats is very real. In the southern states, there is the threat of alligators and wild boar. In most

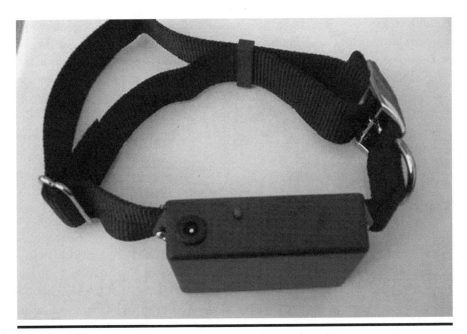

Figure 3.5   Sample Pet Tracker Collar. http://www.surveillance-equip.com/pet. gps.html.

states, small pets are vulnerable to hawks, owls, and other carnivorous birds. Perhaps the greatest threat is the automobile. Finding the remains of a pet after being captured by a carnivore or finding the carcass of a pet on the roadside after being killed by a car would provide closure to the owners. However, the experience of trying to locate the pet may be more traumatic than losing the pet in the first place.

Other Applications

There are many other tracking applications that involve variations of the uses of RFID and sensor technologies. Many states and municipalities track certain criminals out on parole, bail, or emergency home leave. These individuals wear a tracking device in the form of a bracelet on their ankle, and are tracked using geofences and alerting software. Officers of the court systems can track the criminals in real-time, and are alerted when the individuals wander outside the geofence established for them.

Two companies, DriveOK and GPS Teen Tracking, use GPS devices that are placed in vehicles and tracked using GPS technology. These technologies can track the location of the vehicle, the speed of the vehicle, and the time the vehicle stayed at any specified location. The focus of both companies is the tracking of teenage drivers. The tracking of teenage drivers has significant upsides and some downsides as well. One parent was notified that his teenage son had traveled outside the suburb they live in and went downtown to the local nightspots. The parent traveled downtown to meet his son and confront him when he left the nightclub and returned to the car. To his amazement, his son's best friend and another friend returned to the car without his son. This father had come to find out that his son had "traded" the use of his car for the evening in exchange for the use of the best friend's empty house, where the son had planned a date with his girlfriend. The father learned very quickly that tracking the car did not necessarily translate into tracking his teenage son!

Summary

The tracking of animals, marine life, and people has increased in the last several years as technologies have matured and users have focused on measurable value propositions. Safety and reducing costs are at the forefront of tracking animals from farm to fork. Research and food safety are at the heart of tracking marine life. Locating lost pets, wayward criminals, and teenage drivers all have their own value propositions.

Some industries, such as the pork industry, are undergoing significant change. Technologies such as RFID and wireless sensor technologies enhance the size, yield, and safety of the hogs throughout the pork supply chain. In addition, as the global movement around food safety demands traceability from farm to fork, these technologies enable producers to meet these requirements. The pork supply chain serves as a good example of the major changes that are affecting all of agriculture, and how supply chain professionals can lead change in one of the slowest changing industries.

As we have examined in this chapter, the tracking of living beings and the remote monitoring of their environments go hand-in-hand. There is no one "silver bullet" technology. The combination of RFID and sensor technologies allows for the users to apply the right technology with the right application to get the needed results. The supply chain professional must first understand the need for the application, then select the appropriate technologies.

Notes

1. http://www.thepigsite.com/articles/7/markets-and-economics/1614/world-pork-trade-overview-march-2006.
2. http://www.ers.usda.gov/Data/meatpricespreads/, confirmed with Randy Krueger, Cargill.
3. Conversation with Randy Krueger, Pork Systems Consultant, Cargill Meat Solutions. Discussions in 2007; edited chapter received August 16, 2007 by email.
4. http://www.sonotronics.com/html/applications.html.

5. "Shark Followed on 12,000-mile Trip," CNN, October 7, 2005, http://www.cnn.com/sharkmigration.html; emails received from Dr. Bonfil June 4, June 5, and June 8, 2008 editing and approving text.

6. http://www.rfidsolutionsonline.com/article.mvc/RFID-Tracking-TekVet-Wireless-And-IBM-To-Tag-0001?VNETCOOKIE=NO

7. http://www.tekvet.com; and conversations with TekVet Salesman, August 18, 2007.

8. "RFID for Animals, Food and Farming 2007–2017," http://www.idtechex.com/products/en/view.

9. http://www.bsacforum.co.uk/forums/showthread.php?t=8074.

10. http://animalid.aphis.usda.gov/nais/naislibrary/documents/guidelines/06_PIIWG_NAIS_Swine_Program_Standards.pdf.

11. Ibid.

12. http://www.nlpa.org/pdf/er_nais_subcommittee_final.pdf

13. http://www.hsus.org/pets/issues_affecting_our_pets/pet_overpopulation_and_ownership_statistics/hsus_pet_overpopulation_estimates.html.

14. http://www.surveillance-equip/pet.gps.html.

15. http://www.maps-gps-info.com/gp-trkg.html.

16. Ibid.

Chapter 4

The Media Supply Chain Key Word: Digital

Introduction

The use of technologies that include radio frequency identification (RFID) and sensors is rapidly changing the supply chains of many industries. In Chapter 3, we reviewed how these technologies are affecting the supply chains in the agribusiness industry and the tracking of animals, marine life, and people. However, other technological advances are transforming industries and their related supply chains.

The global media and entertainment industry is huge. According to a PricewaterhouseCoopers report released in June 2007, the global media and entertainment industry will be a $2 trillion industry by the year 2011. The United States will hit $754 billion in 2011, or roughly 38% of the global total.[1]

One segment of the U.S. media and entertainment industry is the home video retail sales. This segment alone generated $10.77 billion in sales in the first six months of 2008, with DVD rentals adding $3.9 billion in revenues.[2] This is the traditional DVD market that most of us know and use as consumers. However, the physical make-up of total sales/revenues is changing rapidly due to changes in technology.

History—VHS and Betamax

During the 1980s, there were many battles being waged in the business world that affected the media and entertainment supply chain. There was Apple versus the

Figure 4.1 Betamax cassette (top) and a VHS Cassette (bottom). Source: http://en.wikipedia.org/wiki/Betamax

personal computer makers with Microsoft, Dell versus the retail channel manufacturers, and IBM versus the world. However, one battle that touched most consumers was the battle between Toshiba's VHS and Sony's Betamax (Figure 4.1). (Authors note: The VHS format was developed by JVC in 1976. Toshiba strategically adopted this format. All references to "Toshiba's VHS" are meant to refer to their *adopted* format and not meant to infer that Toshiba *developed* the VHS format.)

Toshiba took the low road and focused on average quality, cheaper price, and longer playing times with its VHS format. Sony took the high road and focused on high quality with a higher price point for its Betamax format. By 1988, Toshiba benefitted from the fact that the VHS format had 98% of the consumer market and it became the standard movie format.[3]

The debate regarding the winner between Toshiba and Sony in the VHS versus Betamax war continues today. Toshiba's VHS became the consumer standard, yet there were multiple companies competing in this commodity-priced market. It is estimated that even in the peak VHS year of 2000, VHS manufacturers only earned an average of $100 million in profit. Sony, on the other hand, took its higher quality Betamax format to the professional and broadcast markets—markets that valued quality despite the higher prices. In addition, Sony had few if any competitors in the Betamax space. In one year alone, Sony earned over $1 billion in profit from its professional video technologies used in the broadcast industry! So, the winner was...?[4]

This battle had the obvious impact on the media supply chain. The raw materials, assembly of the finished hardware, the distribution of the hardware, and the retailing of the hardware were all impacted on who was buying what format.

Therefore, the winner was not necessarily Toshiba or Sony, but Toshiba *and* Sony. In addition, the winners were joined by their consortium of suppliers, partners, distributors, and retailers.

Introducing the DVD

It did not take long before VHS was replaced by the DVD. Another battle surfaced in the early 1990s between Toshiba and Sony. Two high-density optical storage standards were being developed; one was the MultiMedia Compact Disc, backed by Sony and Philips, and the other was Super Density disc, supported by Toshiba, Time-Warner, Matsushita Electric, Hitachi, and many others. It took Lou Gerstner, the president of IBM, to negotiate between the two groups to come up with a single standard and avoid a costly format war similar to the VHS/Betamax war in the 1980s. The result was the current DVD specification that was finalized for the DVD movie players and DVD-ROM computer applications in December 1995. Philips and Sony abandoned their MultiMedia Compact Disc effort when they received a concession regarding disc damage protection.[5] Industry experts believe that Sony at this point was "0 for 2" in terms of battles won and lost with Toshiba, despite the $1 billion in profit from its professional video technologies for the broadcast industry.

Let us push the fast-forward button to 2008. The marketplace has another Toshiba versus Sony battle. This battle is being waged around the new *digital* videodisc format. The new DVD format holds 4 to 5 times more digital audio and video than current DVD discs. In addition, the new DVD format has the ability to store high definition (HD) programs.[6] There are two large consortiums, anchored by Toshiba and Sony, which are pursuing their own standards.

The Toshiba-led HD DVD group includes NEC, Sanyo, Microsoft, Intel, and Universal Pictures. It is also backed (non-exclusively) by Paramount Home Entertainment, DreamWorks, Warner Bros., Warner Music Group, New Line Cinema, HBO, and Image Entertainment.[7]

The Sony-led Blu-Ray Disc Association group has a star-studded members list, including Hewlett-Packard, Apple, Dell, Panasonic, Sony Pictures, MGM, Walt Disney, Twentieth Century Fox, Paramount Pictures, Buena Vista Home Entertainment, Warner Bros., and many industry players like IBM.[8] The Blu-Ray disc format allows for the writing of data on a layer 0.1 millimeter below the disc's surface. Toshiba's HD DVD standard allows data to be written on a layer 0.6 millimeter below the disc's surface, the same as current DVDs.[9] This appears to be an advantage for Toshiba's HD DVD format. However, the Blu-Ray disc version can hold 25 GB of data, versus 15 GB for the HD DVD format.[10]

In July 2007, Blockbuster began carrying Blu-Ray discs in 1,450 more stores. Blockbuster had carried both HD DVD and Blu-Ray in 250 stores as a test. Both formats continue to be offered in the 250 test stores and on Blockbuster

Online. "The consumers are sending us a message. I can't ignore what I'm seeing," Matthew Smith, senior vice president of merchandising at Blockbuster, told The Associated Press.[11]

Toshiba, recognizing the movement in the marketplace toward the Sony Blu-Ray disc made the decision an easy one. In February 2008, Toshiba abandoned the format, announcing it would no longer develop or manufacture HD DVD players or drives.[12]

Although Blockbuster has helped the Blu-Ray disc cause, there was still an issue of price. The HD DVD player costed an average of $250. In mid-2007, with the cost in the $199 range for the Christmas 2007 season, Sony's Blu-Ray players are twice as expensive.[13] If Sony continues to be significantly more expensive than Toshiba, the DVD war could last for years. It would also open up the corporate market to Toshiba—a market that is hypersensitive to price. What a role reversal – Sony chasing the consumer market, with Toshiba possibly ending up the winner in the corporate market. We wonder who will be the winner in the profit wars when the replacement technology emerges for the new *digital* DVD format!

Supply Chain Implications

Now that Sony is the winner of the new DVD war, the net result will be an increase in complexity in the DVD supply chain—but not as dramatic as one with an additional format. The movie studios are releasing movie titles under only two DVD formats: the current DVD format and the new Blu-Ray format. This means that the DVDs must be manufactured with different glass masters, contributing to a proliferation of stock-keeping units (SKUs) in the manufacturing plants. At the retailer level, there will also be a proliferation of SKUs for DVDs, contributing to a greater number of overages, shortages, and returns as supply and demand balance out store by store. The complexity of the two-tier DVD supply chain is complicated (and complimented) by the two-tier DVD player/recorder and the two-tier DVDROM computer applications supply chains. Until the old format diminishes over time, retail stores will have to carry both formats.

Change Is Pervasive

The changes in DVD manufacturing and distribution are significant. However, the home video retail sales business, expected to be $21.9 billion in 2011, is only 1.1% of the total global media and entertainment business. Technology is affecting virtually all segments of this broader industry category.

The music industry encompasses companies that record, publish, produce, distribute, and market recorded music. Technology affected the music industry in a negative way in the early 2000s, when file sharing through companies like Napster created a market to access recorded music without paying a price (royalty) to the rights owners of the recorded music. Judicial decisions to protect the rights owners of recorded music have allowed for the re-launching of file sharing companies as subscription-based service companies.

The re-launching of Napster 2.0 by Roxio and the launching of iTunes by Apple (in 2003) brought a new dimension to the music industry—digital downloading. Individual songs could be downloaded for as low as 99 cents along with customized ringtones for cell phones, with the ownership rights fully protected. By 2005, the impact on the music supply chain was profound.

In 2005, the total value of digital music (downloads, subscription, and mobile) in 2005 was $1.1 billion. The total value of digital music is expected to increase to $4.95 billion by 2010.[14]

The supply chain professional must manage the decline in physical retail sales while encouraging the sales of digital music. This two-tier supply chain network can be tricky, especially when physical hardware (CDs, etc.) is needed to accommodate digital downloading. In addition, the pricing component of supply chain management increases in importance, especially taking into account new releases and special promotional events such as concerts.

The digital downloading of movies and TV shows lags behind the digital downloading of recorded music. In 2005, the digital downloading of movies totaled $11 million, and it is expected to grow to $651 million by 2010. The digital downloading of TV shows totaled $199 million in 2005, and its expected total in 2010 is $2.191 billion.[15]

Wal-Mart stores made significant moves to manage this two-tier distribution of digital content with its online movie download store. Launched in February 2007, this online store sold digital versions of 3,000 films and television episodes from all major studios and selected TV networks. Wal-Mart worked with the studios to price the downloaded movie and TV content in line with prices for the physical DVDs. Their approach was a "product family" pricing approach, which encompasses the physical DVDs and the digital downloads of the content. Wal-Mart's competitor in this space, Apple's iTunes, unencumbered with the carrying of physical DVD inventory, prefers to sell its content with one price. This is regardless of the content being new releases or older titles. With Wal-Mart commanding approximately 40% of the DVD market share, studios were eager to work with Wal-Mart and establish the basic details behind the download service before working with other download services.[16] However, in December 2007, Wal-Mart closed their DVD download store after Hewlett-Packard, which provided the software running the site, "made a business decision to discontinue its video download-only merchant store service." In November 2007, Time Warner's AOL also scrapped its pay-for-download movie service.[17] Insiders from both companies said the download movie volume just did not equal the music download volume, and did not justify the fixed investment to support a two-tier supply chain distribution system. We believe there is enough volume to support a few companies such as Apple's iTunes store and Amazon.com's

Unbox service. However, unless Wal-Mart took their service one step further and had their downloads work on standard DVD players, they would have to work with a diminished market size. Then again, what is a "standard DVD player"?

One segment of the global media and entertainment industry that is growing at a rapid rate is video games. The global video game market is expected to grow at an annual rate of 9.1% to $48.9 billion in 2011, led by Asia with $18.1 billion and 10.0% growth rate. The United States is expected to realize $12.5 billion with a 6.7% growth rate. The fastest growth is expected in the wireless category, with overall growth rates exceeding 20% in each of the major trading blocs. The newest generation of phones that are Internet enabled allow for the downloading of games and other content on an on-demand basis.[18]

In the Eye of the Storm—The Consumer

In the eye of this digital media supply chain storm is the consumer. Experts agree that the supply chains of the past that focused on the distribution of content after it was created are being inverted to focus on the consumer. This is a profound change for the entire industry. Let us take a look at two companies and how they are trying to take advantage of this change by adopting different business models in their respective organizations.

Starbucks—More Than Just Coffee

Ever wonder why people frequent Starbucks with the passion and commitment usually dedicated to a favorite pastime? In early 2007, customers visited Starbucks more than 40 million times *each week* through their 12,440 stores in 37 countries. Starbucks' revenues were $7.8 billion in 2006, a 22% increase overall and the fifteenth consecutive year of comparable store sales growth of 5% or more.[19]

A discussion with one of their senior executives raised a few very telling beliefs that fuel this customer loyalty. This senior executive spoke of "the coffee house experience," "the customer experience," "the human connection," and "the third welcoming place" beyond work and home. In addition, this senior executive spoke of the coffee experience, corporate social responsibility, and innovation.

However, one item surfaced beyond all others. This senior executive said that the Starbucks' customer obviously has the disposable income to buy a premium-priced cup of quality coffee. As such, they believe that this customer also has the disposable income for other items that round out the coffee house experience. At the top of this list is to become a destination for customers to "discover entertainment." The objective is to increase the overall coffee house experience for their customers—and gain an additional share of their disposable income along the way.

Starbucks has created Starbucks Entertainment, designed to provide in-store music for listening or purchase. In addition, Starbucks owns five "Hear Music" coffeehouses where customers can burn their own customized CDs of the music of their choice. Books and movie DVDs are also available for customers.

It is obvious that the media and entertainment supply chains have become an integral part of the products and services provided by Starbucks to their customers. Digitized content is helping Starbucks extend their coffee house experience with their customers, reinforcing their loyalty to Starbucks and creating additional streams of revenue for all companies involved.

Best Buy

If there is one company that stands to lose the most (other than Wal-Mart) with the convergence of technologies and digital content, it is Best Buy. The Best Buy business model has always been around individual products. When one walked into a Best Buy a few years ago, one would walk through games, music, and DVDs to get to computer equipment, electronics, accessories, or televisions. For Best Buy, there have been changes in their operating model because of these technological changes.

Best Buy now has its Magnolia Home Theater Center inside their stores. The Magnolia Theater Center helps customers put together their own home entertainment centers, complete with all the necessary hardware, software, and peripherals. Best Buy's workers help with version control issues as they relate to integrating all the components, and advise existing customers how and when to upgrade items as technological advances occur. It is the home entertainment system they are customizing for their customers, not just selling televisions.

Best Buy created a centralized location for computer repairs, installations, and other services under the banner of "Geek Squad City." The services are price-competitive, and response times are very short. In addition, these locations provided a "pooling effect" for the talent necessary to support a services business. Previously, each store had to rely on its own pool of talent. Supply of the talent, demand for the services, and employee turnover combined to provide significant challenges for Best Buy in satisfying its customers.

The focus of Best Buy is now around developing a long-term relationship with the customer. They have worked at simplifying the complexity of managing through the endless upgrades and versions of hardware, software, and even DVDs for their customers. They have even gone so far as to offer their customers "HD Done Right," a program that offers customers who purchase a flat-panel TVs 37 inches or larger installation and an upgrade to a high definition source. It was only five years ago that customers like us would buy a wireless router with wireless adapters for the home, only to be on our own with Linksys to figure out how to make it all work.

Apple, iPod, iTunes, iPhone

Apple is the company showing the most success in adapting its products and business practices to the digital supply chain. The company has always been the darling of creative media types, providing tools for musicians, designers, and other media content creators ever since the original McIntosh was released. However, Apple's moves since the launch of the iPod in 2001 and iTunes in 2003 have dramatically increased their influence in the digital supply chain. For example, as of July 2007, over 3 billion songs had been downloaded from the iTunes Store, making it by far the most successful "paid-for" music service.

Far from being restricted only to audio, Apple has added TV shows, full-length movies, and podcasts to the iTunes Store, creating a one-stop shop for all types of digital content. The ease of use, polished presentation, and huge lead in sales has made Apple's iTunes Store the player to beat in the digital media market.

Apple is clearly descended from other retail giants in their desire to control the entire buying experience and the "behind the scenes" supply chain. From the days of the Sears, Roebuck catalog to today's master retailers such as Wal-Mart and Target, companies have always wanted to exercise tight control of the process and products sold under their retail brand. However, in today's digital world, Apple has taken the level of control to new heights—controlling not only the retail storefront (iTunes and the iTunes Store) but also the way the product is consumed (only through iPods, Apple TV, and iPhones in proprietary Apple formats). How was Apple able to pull off this feat in the notoriously greedy and paranoid world of big media? In short, simplicity of design is the key.

Apple exercises a clear design aesthetic that informs all of its moves in the digital supply chain. From the clean interface of iTunes, to the simple pricing of music, all the way to the spare and elegant design of consumer devices such as the iPod and iPhone, Apple seems to focus as much on what not to include in these products as it does on what needs to be in them. The results speak for themselves: competitors' products seem bloated with unnecessary features and, in addition, complex to use; and Apple has gained a lead that, for the near future at least, seems insurmountable.

Apple's success provides clear lessons in strategic thinking about how value is brought to customers. First, to enforce their vision, Apple has sought to control the value chain to the greatest extent possible. Their proprietary formats and proprietary content players not only help them differentiate, but also provide some needed comfort to content providers nervous about digital media rights. Second, Apple used pricing, especially in the early days of the iPod, to help customers make the leap into an unfamiliar way of buying content (buying only the bits not the atoms). The 99 cents across-the-board price for songs was brilliant in several ways: it was simple to understand, it was low enough to be a "so what" for many consumers, and it was flexible in allowing consumers to buy individual songs, not the entire albums that dominated the market for years. Finally, Apple has been exhibiting a clear long-term strategy in expanding the range of digital media (music, TV, movies) and the ways the customer can access them (iPods, Apple TV, iMac, iPhone), so that the company stays right at the center of the customer's digital media lifestyle.

Apple has also been very active, albeit indirectly, on the content creation side of the equation. With the sale of animation pioneer Pixar to Disney in 2006, Steve Jobs joined the Disney board of directors and become one of their largest shareholders. Perhaps this loosely coupled arrangement between digital media software (Disney/Pixar) and hardware (Apple) is Jobs' solution in how to link the two spheres where so many others (Sony in particular) have failed.

Perhaps the biggest sign of Apple's huge ambitions in the digital media world is the evolution of iTunes, the free program that was first released for the Mac in January 2001 and for Windows in October 2003. iTunes is the hub of Apple's digital supply chain. It is the place you go to acquire new content whether you are buying from the iTunes Store or ripping (legally) content from previously purchased CDs. iTunes is also the way Apple keeps content providers satisfied by performing digital rights management (DRM) on the music, TV programs, and video you buy, restricting their use to a limited number of devices, while allowing you to share them between your PC or Mac, TV, and iPod.

However, the real hint at Apple's future was the upgrade of iTunes that coincided with the release of the iPhone in June 2007. First, iTunes is the vehicle for activating a new iPhone, a sure sign of Apple's power since all wireless carriers jealously guard their customers. Second, and perhaps more importantly, is the role of iTunes in the ongoing use of the iPhone. It goes without saying that iTunes is used to synchronize digital content to the iPhone by taking advantage of its iPod features. Nevertheless, the new iTunes is also able to synchronize other types of data, including email, address books, and calendars—both on Windows PCs and Macs. This two-way syncing of all types of content means that Apple can connect your device (iPhone), your computer (Mac or PC), and a service (iTunes Store or the Mac SaaS offering), creating a role for them not only in your digital lifestyle for entertainment, but also in your business life.

Pulling It All Together

The digital supply chain encompasses DVDs, DVD players and recorders, digital music, handset manufacturers, retailers, and software providers. The movement of video, music, games, and other content can be challenging. The technological advances happen so fast, they drive the creation of new hardware and software almost overnight. This creates the never-ending "version control" issue that we all face in our everyday lives. One company has attempted to "pull it all together" in a business-to-business media supply chain. This company is called Media Publisher.

Media Publisher (now Qumu, Inc.) was launched in 2000 in Silicon Valley. It provides live video webcasts, video on demand, and digital signage to global Fortune 500 companies. Media Publisher's enterprise software enables their corporate customers to enhance their corporate communications, sales and marketing, training, and human resources (HR) activities. There are numerous companies providing similar services to the marketplace. What makes Media Publisher stand out from its competition is its holistic approach to the digital supply chain.

There are five components to Media Publisher's digital supply chain. These five components are content creation and aggregation, content management, content publishing, content distribution, and reporting.

Content creation is a large, specialized area. Movie studios like Warner Bros., Universal Pictures, and Disney create the most "visible content" to the average person. These studios make the movies we watch at movie theaters, on DVDs in our home entertainment centers, and on our iPods. Music studios like Warner Music produce music, while other companies produce content such as games. There are media outlets such as TV stations, like ESPN (television and radio), that produce live content such as news and sports scores for viewing on television, listening on radios, or both on iPods.

Media Publisher focuses on business-to-business content creation from a different perspective. They provide the software and tools for business content authors to produce, edit, archive, and synchronize their content for their specific audience. One key differentiator is the emphasis by Media Publisher to embrace existing presentation capabilities (PowerPoint, Excel) so that presenters do not have to change how they present. This helps the presenter focus on the content, not the presentation style. In addition, Media Publisher allows their authors to edit post events and to poll audiences to continuously improve the authors' content.

Content management is a critical component of the digital supply chain. Media Publisher aggressively manages a "Master Library" of content through a series of status controls, activity reporting, and expiration dates. In addition, the all-important "access rights" are managed from a central control point. This allows for access on demand from the right people, and a barrier to access (with bread crumbing for tracing non-authorized access attempts) from the wrong people.

Content publishing involves the use of template standards to ensure each portal page contains standard design elements that can be customized by an authorized user. This includes personalization capabilities for the individual as well as "white-branding" for channel customers.

Content distribution is a crowded field in the marketplace. Hardware and software providers have flooded the market, hoping to be part of the entire digital supply solution when adopted by a corporate entity. Their actions contribute to a never-ending integration challenge. Media Publisher unifies video events and programs into a single system. At this step in the supply chain, it is critical that the content can be distributed and accessed remotely, often to locations with varying distribution topologies. Media Publisher recognizes the dangers of providing single-point solutions, and offers their customers pre-built integrations with Cisco, Blue Coat, Stratacache, and Windows Media environments.

Reporting capabilities focus on the value delivered by the user of the digital supply chain. Performance results, such as "who has watched what for how long" are very important for sales, HR training, and corporate compliance initiatives. In addition, a holistic approach to the digital supply chain allows users to assess

"What do people want to learn about?," "How many are viewing what?," and "How effective was the investment of my time?"

The benefits to managing the digital supply chain in media publishing are realized on both the business side and the information technology (IT) side. Companies can manage their message consistency simultaneously across geographic regions. They can continuously improve their messaging as feedback is received. In addition, they can reach a broad audience at a fraction of the cost by not incurring travel costs.

On the IT side, there is a significant resource (and cost) savings associated with substituting event-to-event configuration of messaging with an automated system. Perhaps the biggest savings are realized by utilizing a single, integrated platform across the digital supply chain versus integrating multiple single point solutions.

One restaurant chain has utilized the digital supply chain with Media Publishing in a major way. This restaurant chain places an enormous amount of emphasis on food quality. For their standard menu items and new menu items, the home office food quality staff produces video content on food preparation. The food preparation video is segmented by menu item and covers everything from approved food vendors, type and maintenance of ovens, oven temperatures, and the use of food warmers. The turnover rate in restaurants is very high, adding to the challenge of serving consistently high-quality menu items. The use of streaming these videos into individual restaurants for training purposes is augmented by the mandate that all chefs and waiters attend the training sessions. The training sessions are available on demand, making it easy for restaurant managers to schedule the training for their personnel. The value proposition for the restaurant chain is their consistent high-quality food delivery across all their stores, resulting in their ability to maintain their price-premium in the marketplace vis-à-vis their competitors.

Summary

The digital supply chain has risen to the "peak of inflated expectations" (replacing the physical DVD supply chain) and has fallen through the "trough of disillusionment" (Wal-Mart exiting the download DVD business). During the next five to seven years, we believe the digital supply chain will be in the "slope of enlightenment" stage. From growth in the home video market to the re-formatting of the business models of Best Buy, Wal-Mart, and Starbucks to the game-changing innovations by Apple, the digital supply chains will tightly correlate and interrelate with physical supply chains. What we do know is that supply chain professionals need to be focused on both meeting customer expectations and realizing hard value propositions for their companies. This is not an easy task, given the fluidity of the market. Winners will rise to the challenge, while losers will be yesterday's news.

The challenge exists for the market, specifically academia and supply chain professional associations, to produce an environment that shapes the skills of tomorrow's supply chain leaders. Knowledge of the physical supply chain will still be important, but will need to be augmented by knowledge of the digital supply chain. Financial skills to ascertain hard value propositions will be in demand, especially as they relate to cross-functional solutions (e.g., changing store floor layouts or replenishment programs to better meet customer expectations and increase supply chain efficiencies). Most important will be the environment where professionals will learn how to successfully implement change within their organizations and within their extended enterprises. This skill is vastly different from the functional, tactical execution skills taught by most universities. It is the skill that will make the difference for winners taking advantage of the speed of change in the digital supply chain.

Notes

1. http://www.pwc.com/extweb/ncpressrelease.nsf/docid/E042C329AE0289748525730 10051F322.
2. http://www.switched.com/2008/07/24/home-video-sales-and-rentals-strong-despite-recession/
3. Howe, Carl. " The Wall St. Journal's Faulty Conclusion From The VHS-Betamax War (SNE)," *Seeking Alpha*, January 26, 2006. http://ce.seekingalpha.com/article/6178.
4. Ibid.
5. http://en.wikipedia.org/wiki/DVD/.
6. "Four Studios Support HD DVD, Toshiba Says," CNET News.com, November 29, 2004.
7. http://en.wikipedia.org/wiki/HD_DVD
8. http://en.wikipedia.org/wiki/Blu-ray_Disc
9. "Talks Stall Over Next-Generation DVD Standardization," www.asahi.com/english/ Herald-asahi/TKY200505140123.html, May 15, 2005.
10. http://en.wikipedia.org/wiki/Blu-ray_Disc.
11. http://www.newsvine.com/_news/2007/06/18/787346-ap-blockbuster-to-favor-blu-ray-hd-disc.
12. http://en.wikipedia.org/wiki/HD_DVD.
13. http://blogs.business2.com/utilitybelt/2007/06/bluray_vs_hd_dv.html.
14. http://www.emarketer.com/Reports/All/Em_downloads_jan07.aspx?src=report_head_info_reports.
15. Ibid.
16. "Wal-Mart Launches Online Movie Download Service," http://www.foxnews.com.
17. http://www.msnbc.msn.com/id/22413031/.
18. http://www.businessweek.com/innovate/content/jun2006/id20060623_153211.htm.
19. Starbucks Corporate Fiscal 2006 Annual Report, To Our Shareholders, 4.

Chapter 5

From Sea to Shining Sea: The Changing World of Ocean Container Shipping

Roll on, thou deep and dark blue ocean,—roll!
Ten thousand fleets sweep over thee in vain;
Man marks the earth with ruin,—his control
Stops with the shore.

George Gordon Noel Byron, *Childe Harold's Pilgrimage*

If fishes were wishes the ocean would be all of our desire.

Gertrude Stein

Introduction

The world of ocean container shipping is a complex one that involves companies, countries, politics, and significant costs. Many global supply chain professionals try to simplify their approach in dealing with the complexity around ocean container shipping by outsourcing it entirely to a third-party logistics provider or a freight forwarder. Although the action using a third-party logistics provider may bring with it lower costs on the ocean freight, it may not bring with it lower costs from a door-to-door or full supply chain perspective.

The ocean container shipping industry is being transformed in numerous ways. This transformation is being driven by (among other factors) investments into massive ship sizes, port congestion around the world, growth in containerized cargo, restrictions with the Panama Canal, eco-friendly fuel efficiency initiatives, and of course terrorism. It is critical to understand the basics of this industry to appreciate the impact of technology to address these transformational factors and harness the ever-increasing costs of transport.

The "Container" in Ocean Container Shipping

There are two basic sizes of containers used in ocean container shipping. These two sizes of containers are TEUs (20-foot equivalent units) and FEUs (40-foot equivalent units). Professionals in the industry will commonly refer to these sizes of containers when they are discussing volumes to be shipped. (The United States uses 45-foot containers on domestic routes, but they are not very efficient for global commerce.)

For shippers, it is important to convert TEU and FEU into volume metrics (tare weight, cubic capacity, and payload). Tabe 5.1 provides this conversion.

The "Ship" in Ocean Container Shipping

Containers are placed on container ships. The original objective in using standardized container sizes was to minimize the time in port. Currently, the whole maritime transport industry (ships, ports, etc.) is designed around these standardized container sizes. The size of the ocean container ships used in ocean container shipping ranges from small vessels (<1,000 TEUs) that have their own loading and unloading cranes to large vessels (14,500 TEUs) that rely on cranes at the ports to assist in the loading and unloading of the containers.[1] In 2007, the Maersk Line out of Denmark owned the largest container ships in the world. However, this situation is very fluid and rapidly changes as competitive demands push lines for larger ships (Table 5.2).

Port Congestion and Necessity of Cargo Control

Containers are brought to the ports to be loaded onto the ships. An average port handles thousands of containers a day with a total value ranging from $250 million upwards to $1 billion. The control of the containers in the port is critical to the flow of goods in the global supply chain. Lack of control in the port can contribute to lost containers through misrouting, theft, storm accidents, and (believe it or not) even being dropped into the water due to poor crane handling.

Table 5.1 Standard TEU and FEU Volume Conversions

		20' Container "TEU"		40' Container "FEU"		45' High-Cube container	
		Imperial	Metric	Imperial	Metric	Imperial	Metric
External Dimensions	Length	19' 10½"	6.058 m	40' 0"	12.192 m	45' 0"	13.716 m
	Width	8' 0"	2.438 m	8' 0"	2.438 m	8' 0"	2.438 m
	Height	8' 6"	2.591 m	8' 6"	2.591 m	9' 6"	2.896 m
Interior Dimensions	Length	18' 10 5/16"	5.758 m	39' 5 45/64"	12.032 m	44' 4"	13.556 m
	Width	7' 8 19/32"	2.352 m	7' 8 19/32"	2.352 m	7' 8 19/32"	2.352 m
	Height	7' 9 57/64"	2.385 m	7' 9 57/64"	2.385 m	8' 9 15/16"	2.698 m
Door Aperture	Width	7' 8 3/4"	2.343 m	7' 8 3/4"	2.343 m	7' 8 3/4"	2.343 m
	Height	7' 5 3/4"	2.280 m	7' 5 3/4"	2.280 m	8' 5 49/64"	2.585 m
Volume		1,169 ft³	33.1 m³	2,385 ft³	67.5 m³	3,040 ft³	86.1 m³
Maximum Gross Mass		52,910 lb	24,000 kg	67,200 lb	30,480 kg	67,200 lb	30,480 kg
Empty Weight		4,850 lb	2,200 kg	8,380 lb	3,800 kg	10,580 lb	4,800 kg
Net Load		48,060 lb	21,600 kg	58,820 lb	26,500 kg	56,620 lb	25,680 kg

Source: http://en.wikipedia.org/wiki/Containerization#Dimensions_and_payloads.

Table 5.2   Biggest Container Ships in the World, Listed by TEU Capacity

Year Built	Name	Length o.a.	Beam	Maximum TEU	GT	Owner/Flag
2006	Emma Mærsk	397.7 m	56.4 m	14,500	151,687	Maersk Line/ Denmark
2007	Eleonora Mærsk	397.7 m	56.4 m	14,500	151,687	Maersk Line/ Denmark
2006	Estelle Mærsk	397.7 m	56.4 m	14,500	151,687	Maersk Line/ Denmark
2007	Evelyn Maersk	397.7 m	56.4 m	14,500	151,687	Maersk Line/ Denmark
2006	Georg Mærsk	367.3 m	42.8 m	10,150	97,933	Maersk Line/ Denmark
2006	Gerd Mærsk	367.3 m	42.8 m	10,150	97,933	Maersk Line/ Denmark
2005	Gjertrud Mærsk	367.3 m	42.8 m	10,150	97,933	Maersk Line/ Denmark
2005	Grete Mærsk	367.3 m	42.8 m	10,150	97,933	Maersk Line/ Denmark
2005	Gudrun Mærsk	367.3 m	42.8 m	10,150	97,933	Maersk Line/ Denmark
2005	Gunvor Mærsk	367.3 m	42.8 m	10,150	97,933	Maersk Line/ Denmark

Source: Answers.com, Container ship. http://www.answers.com/topic/container-ship; Largest Ships, 2007.

In the late 1970s, there was an effort by a major industrial company to solve a mystery. They had lost three heavy-duty forklifts on three successive ships that arrived from the Far East. A group of us went to the port to observe the unloading of the fourth forklift and carefully map its progression through the port, through customs, and onto the surface transportation trailer to try and figure out where the forklifts were being lost. It did not take us long.

We watched the container with the forklift being lifted off the ship by a crane. The crane swung the container off the ship toward the unloading dock when the cables slipped, dropping the container with the forklift into the bay. We quickly secured a diver and a recovery team to pull the container with the forklift out of the water. Hours later, when a container with the forklift was pulled out of the water, we discovered that the container with the forklift was not the one that was dropped in the water. It wasn't even one of the forklifts ordered by the industrial company! When the recovery crew was done, 14 containers including 11 forklifts were pulled from the water. The pulleys on the crane were stressed and needed to be replaced. It wasn't so much the weight of the container with the forklift but the weight dispersion of the forklift inside the container that caused the problem with the worn pulleys. The port was so busy that no one had taken the time to stop and maintain the crane. (Why anyone didn't try to recover the containers dropped into the bay before our team came on the scene is beyond us.)[2] Although true, the above scenario is not the norm. The new generation of twist-locks on the cranes used in ports have addressed this specific problem. It is much more common to have ships lose containers in violent storms on the open seas than it is to have them dropped in the water at port.

Failure to manage the throughput of containers in the port, either through mismanagement, labor strikes (longshoremen), or through stress on the port infrastructure from being at over-capacity can wreck havoc on the global supply chain. One has to look no further than the year 2002 to understand the supply chain impact of work stoppages in ports.

October 2002—The Month the Cargo Stopped Moving

In October 2002, 29 West Coast ports in the United States stopped operating for 10 days. The International Longshore and Warehouse Union (ILWU), the union that represents port workers, and the Pacific Maritime Association (PMA), which represents ocean carriers and terminal operators, disagreed on the implementation of barcode readers and GPS technology. The PMA had used these technologies for years in ports worldwide. The ILWU claimed that this technology would eliminate jobs. Management essentially "locked out" the workers while an agreement was being negotiated. The ILWU essentially conceded the use of the barcode and the GPS technologies in return for substantial wage and benefits increases (approximately 25%). However, President George W. Bush had to invoke the Taft–Hartley Act to end the lockout and bring the workers back to work.[3]

The impact was substantial to global supply chains. Factories closed, premium transportation costs were incurred by re-routing cargo to other ports, and store shelves were shorted. Companies accustomed to just-in-time deliveries thought they were prepared for any disruption by carrying up to one-week's worth of supplies. Many of these companies learned a hard but valuable lesson regarding contingency plans. The lockout served notice to supply chain professionals that they need to be prepared with contingency plans that involve the complexities of global supply chains. This includes a review of their outsourcing operations and the use of "dry runs" with their contingency plans and their supply chain partners. The dry runs are critical due to the continuing possibility of future union problems with the congested west coast ports of the United States.

Port Congestion—A Growing Problem

In addition to continuing union strife issues, there is also the issue of congestion itself. The amount of freight inbound into the west coast ports far exceeds the current capacity of these ports to handle the volumes.

We discussed the massive size of the newer ships (up to 14,500 TEUs) that help the shipping company's economics but wreck havoc on the existing port infrastructure. These ships can travel from Asia to the west coast of the United States in approximately 12 days. However, as mentioned earlier, it can take up to 3 days to unload these massive ships.

There is another dimension of managing congestion in the ports. This dimension is one of speed or throughput, the same dimension that exists with surface transportation and distribution center operations. The faster freight can be unloaded from ships and sent to their inland destinations, the more freight a port can handle. Increasing the speed of the throughput of inland freight operations increases the capacity of the port.

In addition to the physical unloading time from the ship, containers must be "processed" in a marine terminal, go through customs, and be sent to an in-bond warehouse or an inland free-trade zone distribution center. The paperwork must match, along with verification that the cargo is compliant with all government laws (including customs and border protection and Homeland Security in the United States).

Currently, large shippers shipping to large consignees that are both known to law enforcement and customs agencies around the world get preferential services in the form of expedited customs pre-clearance. These law enforcement agencies perform a statistical probability analysis on assessing risk by container by trip. There is pressure to increase the sampling of high-risk containers for inspection, but more on this later in the chapter.

In addition, everything always comes down to economics. A ship waiting in a port can cost its operators as much as $300,000 per week in salaries and fuel.[4] Just as airplanes are made to fly and trucks are made to roll, ships are made to sail. Transportation assets need to be moving to earn revenues for their owners and operators. It is critical to get the ships unloaded and reloaded to maximize the number of revenue-producing trips per year.

Growth in Containerized Cargo

Ocean container shipping experts believe that freight shipped by container will increase two- to three-fold (200% to 300%) during the next couple of decades.[5] In addition, as countries such as Mexico and China increase product costs, other countries such as El Salvador and Vietnam will become the de facto choice to produce low-cost products. This will continue the shifting of origins for the ocean container shipping cargo. (The wild card in this scenario is of course the price of oil. If a major disruption in supply would occur causing the cost of oil to dramatically increase, the resultant increase in transportation costs may shift some low-cost manufacturing goods back to destination continents such as North America and Europe.)

Panama Canal

The Panama Canal is rich in history. It was opened in 1914, connecting the Atlantic and Pacific Oceans through the beautiful country of Panama. The Panama Canal was operated by the United States from 1914 through December 31, 1999, when it was transferred to the country of Panama. The Torrijos-Carter Treaty, signed in 1977 between the United States and Panama, provided the political framework for this transition. The Panama Canal is approximately 50 miles (80 kilometers) long. It uses a system of locks that raise the ships to 85 feet above sea level to allow the ships to sail from one end to the other.[6] (See Figure 5.1 for a picture of ships going through the Gatún Locks in the Panama Canal.)

The Panama Canal is very important to international trade and the ocean container shipping industry. There are only two primary routes for ships to travel from Asia to the United States: through the Panama Canal or through the longer distance Suez Canal. The Panama Canal is much shorter, but has a limitation of handling ships with a maximum of 3,600 TEUs. In addition, in 2008, the Panama Canal is operating at 93% capacity. With the newer ships being built to handle 14,500 TEUs and the amount of cargo in ocean container shipping expected to increase two- to three-fold in the upcoming years, the Panama Canal may see a serious decline in its 5% share of world trade handled through its canal unless something is done.[7] (Figure 5.2 shows a couple of container ships going through the Pacific-side locks in Pedro Miguel.)

Figure 5.1　Ships in the Gatún Locks in the Panama Canal.

Figure 5.2   Ships in the Pedro Miguel Locks in the Panama Canal.

The country of Panama and the Panama Canal Authority have a robust plan called the Panama Canal Expansion Program to address this issue. Through this plan, the Panama Canal will expand with a third lane that will accommodate the largest ocean-going ships. (Figure 5.3 shows the basic components of the third set of locks for the Panama Canal.) In mid-2008, pre-construction work began, while the final effort is being made in fundraising and international support. The third lane is scheduled to be open in 2014.[8] Until this third lane is built, shipping companies will have to settle for higher costs associated with alternative routes and smaller vessels to manage the volume of trade from Asia to the United States.

Inland "Ports"

Due to the congestion of the large west coast ports in the United States, several "inland ports" ("dry ports" in the maritime industry) are under development. These inland ports will allow for the diversion of ocean container cargo from Los Angeles and Houston to inland cities for customs clearance and trans-shipment. Cities pursuing inland ports include Chicago, Atlanta, Memphis, Columbus, Toledo, and Indianapolis. Perhaps the two most aggressive cities pursuing inland ports are Dallas and Kansas City (Figure 5.4).

The Inland International Port of Dallas (IIPOD) was established by the City of Dallas, Office of Economic Development. The objective of the IIPOD is to establish

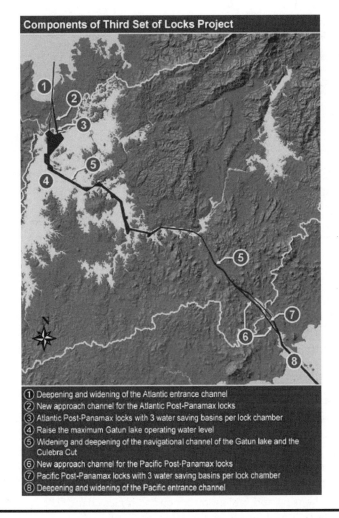

Figure 5.3 The basic components of the third set of locks for the Panama Canal.
Source: http://www.pancanal.com/eng/general/asi-es-el-canal.html

an inland processing center for goods from ships docking at ports in Houston, California, and Mexico. Located in the southern sector of Dallas, the IIPOD has access to five major interstate highways (I-20, I-30, I-35E, I-45, and I-635), a major cargo-handling airport (Dallas/Fort Worth International Airport), three major railroads (Union Pacific, Burlington Northern Santa Fe, and the Kansas City Southern), and two major logistics hubs (Alliance and Dallas Logistics Hub) (Figure 5.5). The International Inland Port of Dallas has signed agreements with the Panama Canal Authority, the Port of Houston Authority, and four Mexican ports (Lázaro Cárdenas, Guaymas, Manzanillo, and Topolobampo) to explore how to utilize the IIPOD when it is fully developed.[9]

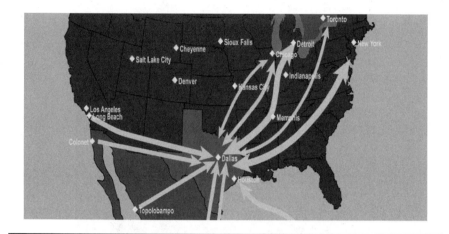

Figure 5.4 Freight flows through the International Inland Port of Dallas.

Kansas City is aggressively pursuing a similar inland port strategy. Kansas City has access to three major interstate highways (I-70, I-35, and I-29), a major international airport (Kansas City International Airport), five railroads (Union Pacific, Norfolk Southern, Burlington Northern Santa Fe, Canadian Pacific, and Kansas City Southern), and a significant trucking infrastructure (YRC Global). Its customs facility is operated by Kansas City SmartPort, and also has a strategic agreement with the Mexican port of Lázaro Cárdenas to divert containerized cargo from the west coast to Kansas City.[10]

The use of inland ports to alleviate port congestion has short-term benefits. It shifts the processing and distribution of imported cargo from congested water ports to open land ports, thus increasing the overall capacity of water ports. However, the use of inland ports has long-term infrastructure implications for the transportation network within the United States. Distribution and transportation lanes change as in-bond warehousing and foreign trade zone activities change the current routings to new routings. (e.g., cargo from Long Beach, California destined for Columbus, Ohio may go through Dallas or Kansas City instead of Chicago, thus changing the transport tonnage balances of two cities—Dallas or Kansas City and Chicago. It also has security implications by virtue of diffusing the inbound "choke points" into the United States.

Security: Secure Freight Initiative and SAFE Port Act

There have been two pieces of legislation in the United States in recent years that have furthered the issue of security in ocean container shipping. In December 2006, the U.S. Departments of Homeland Security (DHS) and Energy (DOE) announced the first phase of the Secure Freight Initiative, an effort to build on existing port security

Figure 5.5   U.P. train going to the International Port of Dallas.

measures by enhancing the ability to scan containers for nuclear and radiological materials at points of origin to better assess the risk of inbound containers. A broad coalition of terminal operators, ocean carriers, and shippers pledged to support this effort at facilities they operate overseas. Six overseas ports are using proven nuclear detection devices and other technologies as part of this initiative. These ports are Port Qasim in Pakistan, Puerto Cortes in Honduras, Southampton in the United Kingdom, Port Salalah in Oman, the Port of Singapore, and the Gamman Terminal at Port Busan in Korea. Containers from these ports are being scanned for radiation and information risk factors are assessed before they are allowed to depart for the United States. In the event of a detection alarm, both homeland security personnel and host country officials will simultaneously receive an alert.[11]

All alarms from the radiation detection equipment for any container will be resolved locally. The U.S. government, the terminal operators, the ocean carriers, and the shippers will work with host governments to establish protocols to ensure a swift resolution by the host government and the prevention of the loading of the container until the risk is fully resolved. At U.S. ports, the DHS has deployed enough radiation portal monitors to scan 80% of all cargo entering the country for radiation.[12]

Two months earlier, in October 2006, the SAFE Port Act was signed into law by President George W. Bush. This act defined a smart container as one that uses a device or system to identify location from origin to destination and to detect a penetration or entry of the container during its movement. (We discussed the door open-and-close capability in Chapter 2.) It also provided a financial return to those who qualify at certain levels of security by allowing expedited treatment through the customs process. This is music to the ears of shippers, consignees, and port operators suffering from the issues of port congestion.[13]

Initial investments in smart containers have focused on radio frequency identification (RFID) applications. The lack of worldwide standards, the overall costs, and issues regarding the placement of readers with mobile assets contribute to an incomplete solution (see Chapter 1). Finally, because of its nature and the control of frequencies by governments, an RFID signal can be the actual means of detonating an explosive device in a container as it is queried at a U.S. port upon arrival by a benign transceiver, appropriately and legally used.[14]

Jim Giermanski, a professor and director of the Centre for Global Commerce at Belmont Abbey College in North Carolina, believes that the solution involves RFID with satellite communications and the use of sensors. He states in his articles that the use of satellite transmissions will avoid the RFID's frequency and protocol limitations, land-based character involving infrastructure costs, historical reporting nature, and the danger when the container holds an explosive device designed to be detonated by a firm's own transceiver in a U.S. port.[15]

We believe there is a balance between the amount of data, the type of data, and the transmission of data over the appropriate communications network. The complexity in door-to-door shipping of containers between countries demands intelligence and the appropriate use of data in the form of meaningful information. We do not agree with the one-size-fits-all communications platform approach. In addition, as we discussed in Chapter 2, satellite transmission costs are high as compared with cellular transmission costs. Who is going to pay for these added costs? As we described earlier, we believe that systems can be economically developed that embrace multiple modes of communication and dramatically lower the overall costs.

The Future: Smart Supply Chain

Precise location tracking of containers and trailers has been around since 1998, while door open-and-close detection capability has been around since 2004. Temperature monitoring of refrigerated containers and trailers (known as "reefers") has been done for years as well.[16] With the introduction of radiation detection and the advances in detecting gases such as carbon dioxide (CO_2), the capabilities are present to elevate a container or trailer to the status of a "smart container" or a "smart trailer."

There are three critical success factors in making a "smart container" a reality. The first critical success factor is to ensure that all the necessary sensors are present in the container to detect mission-critical factors such as temperature, door openings and closures, CO_2, potential toxins, etc. The second critical success factor is to make sure the right device (access point) is designed with the right embedded intelligence and installed on the container to communicate directly with the sensors and the refrigerated unit (if one is present.) The third critical success factor is to design the device to utilize the multiple bands of communications to communicate the necessary sensor data when needed at the lowest possible cost.

Most supply chain professionals will quickly identify a huge missing component to the "smart supply chain." This missing component is the presence of the necessary back-end systems with the right applications to receive and process the data transmitted from the devices on the containers and trailers. These systems have to be "connected" with the installed devices to recognize the devices and receive the data in a common, standardized format. The applications have to process the data from machine-readable to human-readable, and from human-readable to a process-based format. The applications must be able to answer the many questions around "what," "so-what," "why," "how," "whom," and "so now what?" Most supply chain professionals are empowered and compensated to get business results in the areas they are assigned. Data is meaningless until it is translated into the tasks, activities, and processes at hand.

"Smart Container" of the Future

With additional expenses resulting from the cost of oil, the costs associated with port congestion, the costs associated with security, and the costs associated with the current Panama Canal restrictions, the pressure is on for supply chain participants to differentiate their service offerings and command higher rate premiums. One effort underway is to develop the state-of-the-art "smart container" that operates in a "smart cold chain."

Commodities shipped in these reefers range from mutton, kiwifruit, and orange roughy fish from New Zealand to prawns from the Far East to shrimp from the Gulf of Mexico. In addition, numerous pharmaceutical drugs are shipped in reefer containers. The value of the cargo in a reefer container load can easily be in the six figures ($100,000 to $999,999). Small temperature swings can ruin many different temperature-controlled commodities.

Regarding the device or access point, hardware manufacturers in their specialized fields (e.g., Homeland Integrated Security Systems) have worked with other

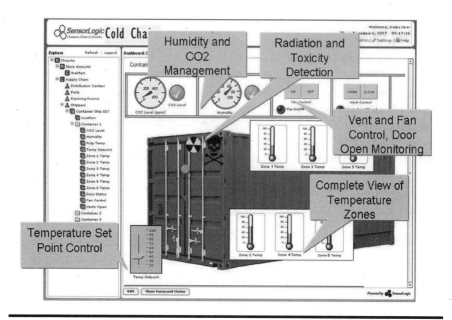

Figure 5.6 The SensorLogic cold chain dashboard. Copyright 2007 SensorLogic, Inc. All rights reserved.

specialized manufacturers (reefer unit manufacturers, sensor manufacturers, and container manufacturers) to produce such a device. It takes a collaboration of many specialists working together to produce the smart container solution.

Software companies such as SensorLogic have developed dashboard prototypes to depict what a smart container solution will look like in the future. Other companies such as Intercontainer have developed end-to-end operational prototypes of the smart container. Sensors in the container will pick up the mission-critical factors (e.g., temperature, CO_2, radiation, toxicity, door open-close, and other readings) for the device to process and transmit the data as appropriate.

The SensorLogic cold chain dashboard (Figure 5.6) provides a good visual depiction for what a smart container can do when outfitted properly with the right sensors, devices, and back-end systems. Although not operational end-to-end, it does show the supply chain practitioner what is possible with the right real-world operational technology.

The ability to identify where the containers are at any given point in time is complemented in the smart container by the ability to identify problem containers. The on-board device will have the computing power necessary to have embedded business rules for every type of sensor. When the sensor readings are detected to be "out of bounds" using the embedded business rules, alarms and notifications will occur. The locations of specific containers can be tracked, with the green containers operating within the embedded business rules and the red containers having one or more problems.

With this solution, the containers with problems can be inquired into by clicking on the icons. The container and the sensor readings can be viewed, along with the diagnosis of the problem. This allows the responsible individuals to take the appropriate actions to correct the issue en-route. In addition, the integration of the container monitoring and control activities with the supply chain applications (order management, transportation management, etc.) can ensure the right decisions are made to protect the deliveries to customers while addressing the problem container and its contents.[16]

Transportation Management Systems and Smart Containers

Smart containers exist in an increasingly global and complex marketplace. Shippers have dealt with longer and more variable lead times, rising fuel costs, changing supply lines, government regulatory mandates, and the threat of terrorism. In many respects, shippers have resigned themselves to be happy with whatever service is provided to them by the transportation carriers.

With the global gross domestic product levels increasing at a decreasing rate, shippers are starting to demand more consistent door-to-door delivery service. Meeting the shippers' expectations in the complex global supply chain is not an easy task. There is the land transportation in the country of origin that can be truck or rail, or both. There is the port of embarkment operations to load the container on the ship. There is the port of dis-embarkment operations and the land transportation in the destination country. Once again, the land transportation can be either rail or truck, or both. The multiple transportation modes and transportation companies participating in the movement of the container pose a significant management challenge to ensure more consistent door-to-door delivery service at a reduced cost.

Supply chain professionals must be active, either directly or with their third-party logistics providers, in negotiating door-to-door carrier contracts, performing network optimization analysis as supply lines and major customers change, and monitoring order execution effectiveness. The order execution effectiveness includes the what-if analysis when service level expectations by transportation carriers are not met.

Perhaps most important on the list for supply chain professionals is the balancing of service versus cost. In many respects, someone in the ocean container world who is responsible for quoting the door-to-door rates to shippers will have a preferred routing to them. This preferred routing may minimize cost but cause the door-to-door delivery service to be entirely erratic. It may route containers to a congested west coast port instead of an alternate port with capacity. In addition, this alternate port may have more direct land transportation options to the container's destination.

The supply chain professional has several software application options to assist him or her in managing the complex global supply chain world. JDA Software Group, Inc. (JDA) has a suite of applications that focus on the movement of the goods to retailers from manufacturers and wholesalers-distributors. JDA has traditional transportation management applications as well from their acquisition of Manugistics in 2006.[17] i2 Technologies, once the undisputed leader in the transportation management systems area, has its total logistics management offering. Several of i2 Technologies's transportation management software modules provide significant value to domestic shippers and selected global shippers.[18]

One start-up company is addressing the need for the next generation of transportation management systems in the global supply chain world. This company is ZMS Technologies, Inc. (ZMS). Founded by Paul Orsak and Dr. Nilendu Jani, ZMS combines constraint-based modeling with real-world business rules to provide transportation management solutions for global supply chain companies. We like how the applications are layered and "fit" the container shipping aspect of the global supply chain.

ZMS has a series of software applications to pull together their customer solutions. The "z! GATE—Global Trans-Modal Routing & Rating" solution is an advanced transmodal routing, rating, and planning engine, encompassing both scheduled carriers (air, bus, LTL [Less-than-truckload], RFS [Road Feeder Service, a truck service to/from airlines for air cargo, rail, ocean] and on-demand providers (couriers, pick up and delivery, TL [Truckload], charter) to allow shippers to consider all options available to them. This is critical for the multimodal aspect of door-to-door shipping with ocean containers. The "z! ENTRY—Order Entry and Quote Management" solution is an enterprise class order and quote entry application module designed to support multiple channels for order capture (EDI [Electronic Data Interchange], XML [Extensive Markup Language—an umbrella term for a way of presenting information in a document that's both computer readable and (in theory) human readable]), CSR [Customer Service Representative] order entry, and customer Web order entry). Working in conjunction with z! GATE, this module presents optimal end-to-end fully rated shipment plans and consists of single and multiple modes. The "z! ORDERx—Order Execution" solution is a configurable transportation shipment execution module designed to automate critical functions and workflows in complex, time definite, or expedited environments. This module includes a flexible workflow engine, supporting various general or unique transportation services and their corresponding activities and milestones. It has a powerful architecture for continuous monitoring, shipment status, workflow management, and settlement activities.

In addition, ZMS has "z! PORTAL—Portal Suite for Customers, Carriers, and Suppliers." This Web-based portal allows shippers to deliver context-based functionality such as order and quote entry, visibility and tracking, profile and rule maintenance, notification services, and financial information. In addition, ZMS has "z! INTEGRATE—Customer, Carrier, and Supplier Integration," an integration hub that supports automated electronic transactions with carriers and agents for tendering, booking, and status monitoring. All of these applications work hand-in-hand with the remote monitoring and control enabler of the smart container. Other ZMS applications include dynamic consolidation, fleet management, sourcing, and business simulation.[19]

Summary

The ocean container shipping world is complex and dynamic. There are numerous operational and technological changes occurring that collectively impact how supply chain professionals approach managing the global supply chain.

Using a combination of RFID and sensor-based technologies, the remote monitoring and control of "smart containers" will be necessary to enable supply chain professionals to meet the challenges into the next decade. These challenges include integrating workflows between order management, warehousing, and transportation; optimizing carrier contract negotiations from an end-to-end perspective; managing the order-to-delivery supply chain from an information, financial, and product basis; and planning and executing when necessary the what-if scenarios to adjust to real-world conditions. The ultimate goals are to reduce total process costs of the shippers' supply chains and maximize the consistency of the door-to-door service. The results will include continuous improvement through exceptional management analysis, better financial controls of freight exceptions (overages, shorts, damages, etc.), and greater control of critical financial performance drivers through the knowledge gathered through remote monitoring and control.

Notes

1. Answers.com, Container ship. http://www.answers.com/topic/container-ship.
2. Fred A. Kuglin, consulting assignment, port of Baltimore, June 1979.
3. http://news.thomasnet.com/IMT/archives/2002/12/the_aftermath_o.html.
4. http://www.eda.gov/EDAmerica/spring2006/shipping_3.html; and discussions with Oliver Martin, October 2007.
5. Ibid.
6. http://www.pancanal.com/eng/general/asi-es-el-canal.html.
7. Ibid.
8. Ibid.
9. http://news.dallaschamber.org/e_article000723736.cfm?x=b11,0,w.
10. http://www.inboundlogistics.com/articles/features/0507_feature03.shtml.
11. http://www.dhs.gov/xnews/releases/pr_1165520867989.shtm, "DHS and DOE Launch Secure Freight Initiative," Release Date: December 7, 2006.
12. Ibid.

13. http://www.homelandsecurity.org/journal/Search.aspx?s=article+155, Satellite Control and the future of Cargo security, April 2007.
14. Ibid.
15. Ibid.
16. http://www.sensorlogic.com; Patrich Simpkins, SensorLogic.
17. http://www.seekingalpha.com/article/25852-jda-software-three-challenges-for-2007.
18. http://www.i2.com/customers/success_stories/.
19. http://www.zmstech.com/what-we-offer.php, and multiple visits by authors to ZMS Technologies with its founders, Paul and Kathy Orsak.

Chapter 6

The Warehouse: Obsolete or a Critical Link in the Modern Supply Chain?

Tilting up his nose,
He inhaled the rancid rosin, burly smells
Of dampened lumber, emanations blown
From warehouse doors, the gustiness of ropes,
Decays of sacks, and all the arrant stinks
That helped him round his rude æsthetic out.

Wallace Stevens, *The Comedian as the Letter C*

We have two sayings at this warehouse: First, we can lose anything. Second, it's a miracle that anything gets there.

Warehouse manager who wishes to remain anonymous

Introduction

Nothing seems so humdrum, commonplace, and outright simple as a warehouse. Goods go in, they are stored for a while, and then selected and shipped out. There is nothing high tech about it—running one of these places would seem to be a "career-ending move," a job for people who cannot do more complex jobs. But nothing could be further from the truth: historically, warehouses have acted as sophisticated players in the supply chain. Today, they serve as critical inventory buffer and switching points that enable highly efficient supply chain operations.

Warehouses: A Very Brief History

One of the earliest forms of written expression is the cuneiform script developed by the ancient Sumerians around 3000 BC and preserved on clay tablets. What is surprising is that in addition to the expected votives to powerful gods and brave kings, there were a much larger number of mundane accounting records like the "warehouse receipt," shown in Figure 6.1, for "29 gur" of barley (whatever a "gur" is).

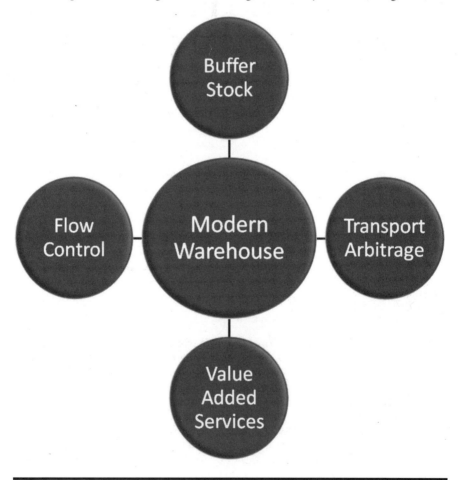

Figure 6.1 Sumerian "warehouse receipt." Courtesy of the Library of Congress, African and Middle Eastern Division, Washington, DC.

In ancient city-states, like those that existed in Sumeria (modern-day Iraq), warehouses were central to the economy and the control that authorities exercised over common people. In an era before banks, the warehouse acted as a place to store value with the currency being tangible goods such as grain.

Over the course of history, warehouses have continued to act as guarantors to the parties involved in buying and selling. This primary purpose survives to the current day and is evidenced by the legal definition of a "warehouse receipt," which is a document that guarantees the existence and availability of a given quantity and quality of a commodity in storage for safekeeping. These receipts are still used in cash and futures transactions to avoid the burden of delivering the physical goods. In some countries, such as Mexico, these receipts must be issued with government assigned serial numbers to aid in tax collection and enforcement.

The modern warehouse has the following functions: inventory flow control, buffer stock management, transport arbitrage, and other value-added services such as kitting, sorting, sub-assembly, store shelf pricing, and many others. At the heart of the warehouse functions is inventory control in the supply chain process from source to sale.

Early Systems for Inventory Control

A long time has passed between the clay tablets of the Sumerians to the current day, but very little changed until the past 50 or so years. (Some might argue that we took a step back from the robust storage media of fired clay to the use of fungible paper.) With the advent of modern computers in the early 1960s, warehouse and inventory control became one of the first targets for computerization. Why were warehouses such early adopters of computer technology? In short, there was a lot of low hanging fruit that could be garnered by implementing a basic inventory management system. As any first-year economics student knows, productivity is the product of labor + capital + technology (know how). Historically, warehouses have been vast consumers of labor (the people needed to muscle physical products around) and capital (the value of the facility, equipment, and the inventory itself). The products of the first industrial revolution—machinery—drove down labor costs by employing more efficient capital goods (forklifts, conveyor systems, racking, etc.) and dramatically increased the amount of inventory that could be physically processed through a warehouse facility. The products of the second industrial revolution—information technology—seek to further reduce the required inputs of labor and capital by substituting technology in their place.

Early warehouse management systems utilized mainframe computers to keep accurate tallies of product flowing in and out of facilities. Hand-written warehouse receipts, pick slips, packing slips, and inventory balances were replaced with accurate computerized records. Control increased dramatically and productivity soared, making possible the modern, consumer-driven retail economy.

False Impression of Warehouses as an Information Technology Backwater

Some people may have the opinion that warehouses are populated by Neanderthals using primitive processes and systems. However, this would be a mistake. Over the past 50 years, warehouses have often been at the forefront of adopting new technologies. Why? Because of the repetitive nature of many warehouse operations and the scale at which they operate, small changes in technology can have breakthrough impacts in performance. Two examples illustrate this fact, the advent of barcodes, and later, wireless computers.

Barcodes and Wireless

Barcodes have become so ubiquitous as to be banal, but if you were born in 1960 or earlier, you can remember when a trip to the supermarket involved a long, laborious checkout process where each price of every item had to be individually keyed in. The barcode was invented by Norman Woodland and Bernard Silver of the Drexel Institute of Technology (now Drexel University) in 1948. They were issued patent number 2,612,994 in 1952.[1]

After some experiments tracking rail cars in the late 1950s, widespread adoption of barcodes had to wait until the early 1970s, when the twin incentives of low-cost lasers and overwhelmed grocery chains teamed up to enable large-scale tests of barcodes in supermarket checkout lines. The Universal Product Code (UPC) was created and individual companies pooled their efforts through the new Uniform Code Council.

Barcodes spread into various industries and back through the supply chain. The UPC standard for product codes was joined by a variety of standards for encoding the manufacturer identity, product lot, and even the individual instance of a product. The most important standards for warehouse use were the Serial Shipping Container Code (SSCC-18) and Shipping Container Code (SSCC-14). SSCC-18 (the 18 being the length of the code) allowed for serialized control down to a unit level, whereas the shorter SSCC-14 is useful for production lots or other aggregations of product.

At last, products, cases of product, pallets of product, and even containers (truckloads) of product could be labeled and uniquely identified with a machine-readable barcode, eliminating a huge amount of manual, error-prone transcription work. Fixed scanners could be mounted at receiving and shipping doors and along various control points on conveyor systems. Warehouse productivity soared once again.

Now roll the clock forward to the 1990s and there's another problem to solve—how to break the "chain" keeping barcode scanners and computers at fixed locations. The answer was radio frequency (RF). This is the not the RF associated with the passive radio frequency identification (RFID) tags so hyped these days and covered earlier in this book, but local RF-based computer networks that allowed hand-carried or vehicle-mounted computers and scanners to roam the warehouse while maintaining communication with the warehouse management system. First deployed as narrow band networks and then using spread spectrum technology, these systems now use standard Wi-Fi–based wireless local areas networks. The combination of these two technologies—barcodes + wireless—was a blockbuster and truly enabled warehouses to achieve "six sigma" levels of accuracy and efficiency. Warehouse operations could now ascend the ladder of operational effectiveness.

Level 1. *Knowing where stuff is:* Achievable before barcodes and wireless, this was the first level of sophistication that computer systems were able to produce.

Level 2. *Directing the action:* With RF, systems could now take control of what individual workers were doing, sending real-time work requests to them and monitoring their completion. Possible, but clumsy with paper-based systems, RF plus barcodes provided mobility, accuracy, and real-time control.

Level 3. *Measurement against standards:* With these technologies and analyses of the workflow within warehouses, it became possible to establish standards for how long tasks should take. A by-product of RF task direction gives the system the start and end times for each task. Measuring against a standard, either individually or for a team, is a simple by-product.

Level 4. *Incentives*: "If you can measure it, you can manage it" is a classic business cliché—but one with much real-world truth. Most warehouse work is monotonous and repetitive, so why not turn it into a game? The system calculates the standard for how long a piece of work should take and broadcasts it to your RF-enabled mobile computer, you complete it, and you get instant feedback. If you do better than standard, a small bonus is added to your paycheck. Consistently perform above standard, and your pay rises substantially.

What Barcodes and RF Illustrate about Technology Adoption

A look at the adoption curve for barcodes and RF should immediately humble any techno-visionary who is pushing the "next big thing." Barcodes took a good 30 years between invention and widespread adoption. Mobile RF for the warehouse took even longer by some measures. The "spread spectrum" radio technology that was so important to widespread adoption in interference-prone warehouses was first alluded to in patents filed by Nikola Tesla in 1900 and later by actress Hedy Lamar and composer George Antheil during World War II. They received U.S. patent number 2,292,387 in 1942 for using spread spectrum in secure radio communications.[2]

When new technology is invented, a variety of other changes must take place to enable adoption. First, people sometimes need to change their attitudes about what is possible or even desirable. For example, tracking to the case level is possible with barcodes and the SSCC-18 standard, but many companies, for a variety of reasons, do not implement it. Second, many breakthroughs often require supporting technologies to make them deployable. For example, barcodes needed the low-cost laser; mobile RF needed the lightweight computer, which in turn needed the microprocessor.

What about RFID?

Some readers may be asking themselves why the hype about RFID when much of the benefits of this new technology can already be garnered with existing, time-tested barcode and RF techniques. The answer is complex, and a trip back to Figure 1.1 in Chapter 1 may provide a partial explanation—technology adoption always seems to follow a path of inflated expectations, followed by disappointment, and later by acceptance and effective use.

Heavyweight promoters like Wal-Mart and the U.S. Department of Defense certainly explain some of the attention. But underneath the fluff of hype there is a truth that any supply chain practitioner understands: small, incremental changes in process make a huge difference in outcome. Nowhere is this more the case than with the modern warehouse. Wal-Mart, for example, wants to dramatically increase the amount of product that moves through its existing warehouse infrastructure over the next few years. RFID makes possible some subtle but important changes in how these facilities operate, thus making the goal achievable. First, the scanning of an RFID tag does not have to be "line of sight" as it does with barcodes. This means that the orientation of the product as it moves through the facility can be more flexible. It also means that workers do not have to leave their equipment to initiate scans. "Toll gates" can be set up at receiving and shipping doors so that any product moving through automatically triggers read-transactions. RFID readers can be installed in storage racks (and store shelves for that matter) so that real-time inventory is always available.

The potential benefits are real because all these little process advantages add up quickly at the volumes that Wal-Mart and the Department of Defense push. So why is adoption taking so long? In addition to the normal adoption challenges of changing people and processes and waiting for complementary technologies to develop, RFID faces a couple of unique issues. First, the idea of tagging everything and having that tag still on the product (and potentially readable) as it left the store triggered many consumer privacy concerns. Second, new technology adoption requires a fair distribution of benefits, and, to date, RFID appears to primarily benefit the big retailers while doing little for the other players. Finally, reading passive RFID tags is actually quite a difficult physics problem. Unlike barcode scanning, where a smart device (a person) aims a narrow focus laser scanner at the desired target, filtering out all sources of "noise," passive RFID with its non-line-of-sight read presents a host of challenges in discriminating the target tags from others nearby also reflecting the signal. Intervening materials in the product or its packaging like water and various metals wreak havoc. These problems will be solved, but the process will involve substantial trial and error and much more time than was originally forecast.

Future of Warehouses

In the quest to become ever more efficient while raising the standard of customer service, warehouses in the supply chain will continue to see many changes in the first two decades of this century. The technology march continues and it is clear that the following trends will impact these operations:

- Material handling advances: The physical movement of product in, out, and around warehouse facilities has advanced greatly in the past 100 years. But sometimes advanced material handling has the hidden cost of reducing flexibility in the operation (types of products that can be handled, packaging limitations, etc.). However, advances in machine intelligence, particularly around machine vision, will rapidly create new opportunities in the next few years for deploying robots to tasks, such as order picking, that currently require people.
- Identification advances: RFID will continue to evolve and, as costs fall, new applications will emerge. RFID "dust" (very small RFID chips) are already finding their way into authentication uses. As RFID combines with micro-sensors, it will soon be possible to track the provenance of a product from the time it leaves the factory until it is brought into your home. Knowing whether a product was opened, dropped, defrosted, heated up, or drenched is obviously important information in certain applications.
- "Green" advances: Warehouses are massive consumers of energy, especially refrigerated facilities. Given the impact of carbon emissions on the global climate, warehouses are clearly targets for energy efficiency improvements. In some countries, such as Germany, warehouses have long been subjected to regulations because of their size and the amount of vehicle traffic flowing in and out of them. This has led to practices requiring the reduction of truck idling time to the construction of special "green roofs" that feature live grass and other plant life growing on them. This practice not only softens the visual profile of these massive structures, but helps cool the building while capturing and sequestering some of the carbon emitted by the transport fleets servicing them.
- Full value chain optimization: Even today, optimally operating warehouses do not necessarily contribute to the overall efficiency of the supply chain because warehouses often operate in isolation from the overall demand and supply signals of the network. As companies increasingly realize that the supply chain is a "many to many" model that needs to be operated holistically, warehouses jump to the fore as a critical part of the equations. If you think of products

flowing through the supply chain like a liquid, warehouses act as flow valves and storage reservoirs helping the entire flow operate more efficiently. As software evolves and supply chain functionality moves the network cloud, warehouses will act as critical providers of real-time data about the chain's ability to react quickly to changes in demand and supply signals. This information will be acted on immediately and replenishments plans, warehouse picking plans, transport plans, and factory production plans will all be dynamically recalculated in response to changes in real-world conditions.

Conclusion: Physical Execution Still Matters

Despite some pundits predicting the "end of the warehouse" with everything moving to only in-time delivery, the warehouse is not going to disappear anytime soon. These facilities serve as the switching points for the supply chain, re-routing product in real time to where it needs to go. Warehouses provide a buffer of inventory for those processes and industries where "just in case" can be as important as "just in time." Warehouses allow for significant reductions in transportation costs, where full truck loads of product from manufacturers can be broken down and mixed into truckloads appropriate for a single store, reducing the number of truck rolls needed to keep the store in stock.

Warehouses have always been early adopters of new technology because of the scale at which they operate and the value of the products flowing through them. Continued advances in computer software and hardware and the application of advanced robotics to material handling will create additional efficiencies. The warehouse of the future is always online, receiving demand and supply signals from partners and providing real-time information on the ability to fulfill demand.

As the global economy becomes more interdependent and supply chains longer and more prone to disruption, the warehouse stands as a vital node in assuring that the right product gets to the right place at the right time.

Notes

1. United States Patent and Trademark Office. See Web site http://patft.uspto.gov/netahtml/PTO/srchnum.htm and key in patent number 2,612,994.
2. United States Patent and Trademark Office. See Web site http://patft.uspto.gov/netahtml/PTO/srchnum.htm and key in patent number 2,292,387.

Chapter 7

Pharmagistics

Counterfeit drugs—illegal and inherently unsafe—are a growing public health problem.

FDA Web site homepage, August 2007

I will not let him stir
Till I have used the approved means I have,
With wholesome syrups, drugs, and holy prayers,
To make of him a [sane] man again.

William Shakespeare, *The Comedy of Errors*

Introduction

The pharmaceutical drug industry is described by many experts as a global industry dominated by large capitalization, research-based multinational companies. Depending on one's definition of the pharmaceutical drug industry (including or excluding pharmacy benefit managers, or PBMs; pharmacy services companies, including retailers; etc.), this industry approaches a *trillion dollars* in revenues. It has size, scale, profitability, and opportunity. (Although some experts believe the size and profitability of the "illegal drug" industry would dwarf the numbers of the legal drug industry!)

In many developed countries, the populations are getting older while the life spans of these populations are increasing. Countries such as Japan and Hong Kong (82 years); Sweden, Switzerland, Australia, France, Iceland, and Canada (80 years); Spain, Italy, Norway, Israel, Greece, Austria, The Netherlands, Germany, Belgium

95

(79 years); and the United Kingdom, Finland, and the United States (78 years) have significant populations with life expectancies equal to or greater than 78 years.[1] In addition, among the countries currently classified by the United Nations as more developed (with a population of 1.2 billion in 2005), the median age of the population rose from 29.0 in 1950 to 37.3 in 2000, and is forecast to rise to 45.5 by 2050. The corresponding figures for the world as a whole are 23.9 for 1950, 26.8 for 2000, and 37.8 for 2050. In Japan, one of the fastest ageing countries in the world, in 1950 there were 9.3 people under 20 for every person over 65. By 2025 this ratio is forecasted to be 0.59 people under 20 for every person older than 65.[2] The combination of rising life expectancy and declining fertility and birth rates will drive significant growth in the global demand for pharmaceutical drugs in the next decade.

Supply chain professionals are starting to be "in-demand" in this industry due to a number of driving forces. First, the managing of manufacturing supply chains for pharmaceutical drugs is a long and complex series of activities. A few pharmaceutical drugs have up to 15 different, discrete value chains and span over 300 days from the start of production to the finished product.[3] Second, the push by healthcare providers to use generic drugs as soon as possible (by setting lower co-payments for generic versus branded drugs) results in increased pressure for supply chain professionals to plan for and manage the transition between branded and generic drugs. Third, the use of existing drugs for new indications or use with other drugs expands markets—and supply chain complexity—for drug manufacturers. Specialty drugs (cancer, multiple sclerosis, arthritis, diabetes, heart disease) are very expensive and frequently need refrigerated transport and warehousing. There is intense pressure from medical providers for suppliers to deliver the needed pharmaceutical drugs (and medical devices) from the source of supply *to the patient,* getting medical facilities out of the distribution business while increasing patient-based percentage order-fill rates. Last but not least, pressure is building for product authentication throughout the total supply chain, eliminating any counterfeit product, illegal diversions of legitimate product, or terror-related incidents. Every one of these market forces could command a book written about them. It is this last item, eliminating counterfeit product from the drug supply chain, that we will focus on in this chapter.

In the pharma industry, several efforts are being made to improve the supply chain performance of manufacturers, distributors, and retailers and elevate the role of the supply chain professional within the industry. One needs to look no further than the LogiPharma Conference to find several executive presentations on the agenda that address specific supply chain issues facing the pharma extended enterprise.[4] The LogiPharma Conference, as conferences go, is a very good one with quality presenters and timely presentation topics.

However, it is our opinion that this conference only addresses the tactical execution of specific tasks facing the pharma industry. Perhaps the industry is conditioned to executing within the myriad of government regulations that control various aspects of the industry and has lost the ability to take the strategic perspective. We believe there are enough serious issues in the pharma supply chain to merit leaders stepping out and defining new practices and processes without waiting for the government to publish new regulations.

It is hard to imagine the large cap, multinational pharmaceutical drug companies *not* being research based, for the lifeblood of these companies rests in their new product pipelines. However, the pipelines of blockbuster drugs are starting to dry up while some of the top-selling drugs in the history of the pharmaceutical industry will have their patent protection expire in the near future. Generic competition is expected to wipe out $67 billion in U.S. sales between 2007 and 2012, or roughly half of the total sales.[5] According to Datamonitor, annual industry revenue will decline between 2011 and 2012. This will be the first decline in annual industry revenue in four decades for pharmaceutical companies.[6] The combination of increasing demand and decreasing revenues will undoubtedly heighten the focus on addressing the threat of counterfeit drugs entering the supply chain. These industry forces are creating the emergence of a critical new competency in the pharmaceutical drug industry, and a new stage for supply chain leaders—*pharmagistics!*

Counterfeit Drugs—The Problem Defined

A counterfeit drug is a medication that is produced and sold with the intent to deceptively represent its origin, authenticity, or effectiveness. A counterfeit drug may be one that does not contain active ingredients, contains an insufficient quantity of active ingredients, or contains entirely incorrect active ingredients (which may or may not be harmful), and which is typically sold with inaccurate, incorrect, or fake packaging.[7]

According to the U.S.-based Center for Medicines in the Public Interest, counterfeit drug sales will reach $75 billion globally in 2010. This is a 90% increase from 2005. It is estimated that counterfeit drugs in most industrialized countries amount to less than 1% of the market value of pharmaceutical drugs. This compares to >20% in the former Soviet republics and as high as 30% in many countries in Africa and parts of Asia.[8]

The tragedy can be tallied in terms of pure numbers. In Niger in 1995, 50,000 people were inoculated with fake vaccines resulting in 2,500 deaths. In the same year, 89 children died in Haiti while 30 children died in India from cough syrup prepared with diethylene glycol, a toxic chemical used in antifreeze. In 1999, 30 people died in Cambodia after taking counterfeit anti-malarial medicines. In 2001, a Wellcome Trust study found that 38% of 104 anti-malarial drugs on sale in South-East Asian pharmacies did not contain any active ingredients.[9] One has to wonder how many deaths go undiagnosed by doctors. In addition, one has to wonder how many deaths were unnecessary or accelerated by counterfeit drugs when pharmaceutical drugs were prescribed to help cure a disease or prolong a patient's life.

U.S. Food and Drug Administration and Product Authentication, 2004

The U.S. Food and Drug Administration (FDA) routinely conducts counterfeit drug investigations. These investigations have been on going for 17 to 20 years. By 2003, these investigations quadrupled, with investigations focused on (among others) the high profile cholesterol-lowering drug Lipitor and Procrit, an anemia treatment used by cancer and AIDS patients.[10]

In response to the dramatic increase in counterfeit drugs, the FDA established the FDA Counterfeit Drug Task Force. The FDA published its first report in 2004, based on the work performed by this task force. This report contained seven major recommendations to address weaknesses in the drug distribution system.[10] The recommendations in this report are as follows:

1. New technologies, including RFID, color-shifting inks, holograms, and chemical markers incorporated into the drug or its label
2. Stricter licensing requirements to shore up state rules for licensing wholesale drug distributors and making it more difficult for illegitimate wholesalers to get into business
3. Tougher penalties to make counterfeiting drugs a crime equal to registered trademark infringement crimes
4. More secure business practices
5. Increased education
6. International collaboration (World Health Organization, Interpol)
7. Improved reporting systems to quickly identify counterfeit drugs, pinpoint how they got into the distribution system, and notify the public of the potential danger

All seven recommendations had value in 2004. To some extent, these recommendations have value in 2008, and some progress was made between 2004 and 2008. (The problem is that the bad guys have made progress as well!) The first, fourth, and seventh recommendations are of special interest to supply chain professional and fuel the movement of pharmagistics. Let us take a brief look at these three recommendations.

New Technologies

Here we go again with radio frequency identification (RFID). In 2004, the FDA encouraged the use of electronic track-and-trace technology to secure the integrity of the drug supply by providing an accurate, electronic drug pedigree called "e-pedigree." A pedigree is a paper or electronic document (e-pedigree) that enables a single view of the product and order and is used for drug authentication (see specific requirements of a "pedigree" below). The pedigree goes with the drug and tracks the change of custody as the drug passes through the supply chain. An example of a pedigree requires signatures verifying the name, address, and date of all prior sales tracing back to the manufacturer.

The requirement of a drug pedigree is not new. The Prescription Drug Marketing Act (PDMA), effective 1988, was enacted amid growing concerns of prescription drug diversion and counterfeiting. Drug wholesalers that are not manufacturers or authorized distributors of a drug must provide a pedigree for every prescription drug they distribute.[11]

The specific requirements of a "pedigree" are as follows:[12]

1. The proprietary and established name of the drug
2. Dosage
3. Container size
4. Number of containers
5. The drug's lot or control number(s)
6. The business names and addresses of all parties to each prior transaction involving the drug, starting with the manufacturer
7. The date of each previous transaction

In essence, the e-pedigree provides an electronic record of the chain of custody of the product as it moves from the manufacturer through the supply chain to the pharmacy. The FDA stated that RFID was a promising technology to achieve an e-pedigree. Based on input received from its members and technology providers, the FDA stated that widespread adoption and use of this electronic track-and-trace technology would be feasible by 2007.

In 2004, the promise of RFID was very high for many industries. (As we discussed earlier in the book, the promise of RFID was *way* ahead of its headlights in terms of *real* value for most consumer packaged goods, or CPG, applications.) However, the authors do believe the use of RFID is a good start to begin to address counterfeit drugs entering the pharmaceutical distribution system.

More Secure Business Practices

If you read the summary of the FDA report, you would ask yourself, "What about secure business practices?" The authors have visited shipping facilities of pharma manufacturing plants, distribution facilities of companies ranging from Cardinal Health to McKesson, and even the reverse logistics and disposal facilities of Carolina Logistics Services, part of Inmar. There are companies that have been doing excellent work in the area of secure business processes since 2004. We congratulate these companies for their efforts. Unfortunately, these companies represent only their part of the drug supply chain. Horror stories about lack of control abound in the pharma supply chain. One of us had a healthcare organization as a client. The company ran its own drug distribution centers and was very proud of its processes and the long tenures of their warehouse employees. After deploying a new inventory control system in the facility, the reason for employee longevity became apparent: poor physical and IT controls were allowing the staff to rob the place blind! The staff could not afford the pay cut to work somewhere else, hence the longevity.

Improved Reporting Systems

The FDA report identified the need to have procedures in place to recognize counterfeit drugs and quickly alert the public to the discovery. Pharma companies agreed to participate in a voluntary program to notify the FDA's Office of Criminal Investigations of suspected counterfeiting within five working days. The FDA also announced the Counterfeit Alert Network, a group of organizations that agreed to "spread the word" about counterfeit incidents. In our opinion, this recommendation of the report was one of the weakest, because it relied more on voluntary cooperation between organizations than disciplined reporting within one shared, secure system.

The Problem Worsens

Since 2004, there have been a number of high profile incidents—and casualties—resulting from counterfeit drugs. In January 2006, the FDA issued an alert about fraudulent influenza remedies, especially counterfeit prescriptions of the Tamiflu medication. The Dutch Inspectorate warned consumers in early 2006 not to buy Tamiflu through the Internet after discovering the counterfeit capsules contained lactose and vitamin C, and no active ingredients. The United Kingdom also seized 5,000 packets of counterfeit Tamiflu in early 2006.[13]

In 2005, the Dominican Republic, El Salvador, Kenya, and Indonesia all performed studies that documented significant issues with counterfeit and stolen drugs. The Dominican Republic's public health department reported that 50% of the country's pharmacies operated illegally, and 10% of all medicines arriving into the country were counterfeit. Indonesia reported that pirated drugs make up 25% of its $2 billion pharmaceutical industry.[14] The list is a long one.

In 2006, the diethylene glycol issue surfaced in Panama with deadly consequences. Government officials unwittingly mixed it into 260,000 bottles of cold medicine. There were 365 reported deaths and an unknown number of related illnesses. The *New York Times* traced the diethylene glycol back to Chinese companies that made and exported the poison as 99.5% pure glycerin. There was no testing done as the material passed through three trading companies on three continents. The reporter discovered no continuity of documents to identify the original manufacturer, and no ability for buyers to track and trace the material.[15]

Fast Forward—October 2006

In June 2006, the Acting Commissioner of Food and Drugs, Dr. Andrew von Eschenbach, published the Counterfeit Drug Task Force 2006 Update to the 2004 study. The findings are as follows.

New Technologies

As we know, 2007 has come and gone, and as we predicted the promise of RFID technology is still just a promise. Many pilot programs were conducted with e-pedigree and RFID that consisted of one manufacturer, one distributor or wholesaler, and one pharmacy. A common critical learning from the pilot programs was the need to adopt mass serialization with unique identifiers on each package to facilitate e-pedigree adoption. Special recognition went to GlaxoSmithKline, Pfizer, and Purdue Pharma for their efforts in tagging their products. However, the FDA went so far as to say they were "disappointed" with the lack of overall progress in the drug supply chain.

Regarding RFID technology specifically, the same issues CPG manufacturers and general merchandise retailers have struggled with for years surfaced among the pharma supply chain participants during these pilots. These issues range from a lack of standards; privacy concerns; data ownership and confidentiality concerns; the lack of definitive data on how well RFID works with liquids, metal, and biologics; challenges in serializing all products; and, last but not least, concerns over the accuracy and speed of electronic RFID devices. We know the FDA and its members had to discover these issues for themselves, but a half-dozen experienced and smart CPG and retail executives could have written this issue summary for the industry without incurring the time or expense in struggling through the pilots. The consensus among pharma supply chain participants is that widespread adoption of RFID is many years away, perhaps as many as ten years.

There has been progress made in this area since 2004. On January 26, 2007, the company T3Ci announced that it was approved for a patent in product authentication. T3Ci, working with EPCglobal and their efforts on electronic pedigree and standards for the interchange of documents, was able to track serialized units of medication after an incident occurred, analyze the movement history, and discover substituted drugs before they were administered to patients.[16]

More Secure Business Practices

The 2006 report identified that the FDA was encouraged by industry participants to implement federal uniform pedigree requirements and standards binding on the drug supply chain and all states. This action would standardize data fields that could capture product information, item information, transaction and trading partner information, and the digital signatures of sellers and recipients. Unfortunately, the U.S. Congress, not the FDA, has the statutory authority to implement such a universal, mandated program.

Without this common product flow data, there will remain a lack of end-to-end connectivity of these disparate supply chain activities. With this common product flow data, the supply chain participants can proactively self-monitor themselves as one ecosystem. We believe that the standardization of the data fields that enable supply chain participants to verify and authenticate the drugs at each entry or exit point in the supply chain, visible within the identified ecosystem by all supply chain partners, would provide a significant barrier for counterfeiters to penetrate once established.

Improved Reporting Systems

One of the FDA recommendations in the 2006 update report is a "no preference" whether a distributed versus central database is used, as long as every entity in the drug supply chain has access to information about a specific product back to the manufacturer. We believe that a distributed database accessible through a common set of Web services is the best route, as long as there are national (and international) standards to implement common product data flow between participants. We can start with national standards to avoid having each state take action to address the counterfeit issue while Congress waits to make a decision.

Privacy issues are real with the use of RFID tags. The FDA has done research in this area, but is still unsure how to address turning "off" RFID tags or educating consumers about the RFID tags.

We believe that waiting for RFID to "mature" into a usable technology on a broad scale is a mediocre strategy at best. We believe there are alternatives to RFID that can address the issue of counterfeit and stolen drugs. However, we need to move fast because both the counterfeit drugs and stolen drugs issues appear to be worsening as time passes by.

Diverted (Stolen) Pharmaceutical Drugs

In October 2006, the National Drug Intelligence Center published its National Drug Threat Assessment 2007 report. The following are the four "Strategic Findings" from this report[17]:

- The availability of diverted pharmaceutical drugs is high and increasing, fueled by increases in both the number of illegal online pharmacies and commercial disbursements within legitimate pharmaceutical distribution chain.
- The implementations of pedigree systems such as RFID could help to eliminate the introductions of counterfeits as well as deter the diversion of commonly abused drugs from the legitimate pharmaceutical supply chain.
- Rates of past year use for pharmaceuticals are stable at high levels.

■ Demand for prescription narcotics may decline as some users switch to heroin, particularly where law enforcement curbs the diversion and availability of prescription drugs.

According to this report, the illicit diversion and theft of pharmaceuticals from legitimate suppliers is high and increasing. The good news is that there has been a reduction in specific geographic areas or states through sustained law enforcement, education, reduced access in pharmacies, and implementation of prescription monitoring programs. The bad news is that these efforts are state initiated, and not implemented on a nationwide basis. (If they work, why are these practices not adopted in all 50 states?) To this end, it is refreshing to see the number of vice presidents of supply chain in the major pharma companies who double as the chief security or chief risk officers for their companies.

In addition, illegal online pharmacies have sprung up like weeds in your lawn after a nice spring rain. (Have you been spammed with special offers for "inexpensive drugs" in the past 30 days?) These illegal online pharmacies promise genuine, low-priced drugs. Sometimes they do deliver expensive drugs at a significant discount because they are authentic and stolen or diverted from the drug supply chain. Sometimes these drugs are very dangerous because they are counterfeit. More than 50% of Internet drug outlets, which conceal an actual address, have counterfeit drugs, according to the World Health Organization.[18] In May 2007, the FDA issued a warning about counterfeit Internet sellers, citing 24 Web sites that are suspected to be distributing counterfeit drugs.[19] Why are the authentic drugs so easy to steal? Where are the counterfeit drugs coming from, and how are they able to get into the overall drug supply chain?

Do Not Forget about Reverse Logistics

One area of exposure for counterfeit and stolen drugs is reverse logistics. A significant number of pharmaceutical drugs (and over-the-counter medication) are processed from their normal retail and wholesaler or distributor channels into "the pharmaceutical drug graveyard." These prescription and over-the-counter drugs that are processed through this channel have exceeded their shelf lives, have been manufactured outside of the mix tolerances, or in some cases represent excess inventory.

The "reverse supply chain" from retailer or wholesaler or distributor to the graveyard or destruction of the drugs can provide ample opportunity for the "bad guys" to tamper with or steal these drugs. Once they have these drugs, they can re-introduce them to the legitimate or illegitimate supply chains. One industry executive told us that the reverse logistics process is a prime source for illegitimate drug sales over the Internet.

Carolina Logistics specializes in the execution of the reverse logistics process for pharmaceutical and over-the-counter drugs through its CLS MedTurn, Healthcare Services Division. CLS MedTurn goes through the seven steps of pedigree documentation from the time it receives the drugs, through the inventory process (waiting on destruction approval), and to the point of product destruction. Special security cages are used for the high-risk drugs. The CLS MedTurn employees are required to go through background checks, to be bonded, and have security clearances for their specific work areas. All the necessary reports are filed and made available to the FDA and other government agencies on a routine basis.[20]

It is unfortunate, because some of these pharmaceutical drugs and over-the-counter drugs are still good when they reach the graveyard. Perhaps some of the drugs reached their retailers without the adequate shelf life to avoid code date expiration with consumers and were rejected. Other drugs that represent excess inventory are still good, but they represent an oversupply and unsaleables due to the imbalance of supply and demand. Whatever the reason why the drugs reached the graveyard, it is important to have the controls in place. These controls prevent well-intentioned people from providing pharmaceutical drugs to the "bad guys" for illicit purposes.

Back to the Future and the FDA 2004 Report

In the 2004 report, the FDA cited use of color-shifting inks, holograms, and chemical markers into the drug or its label as promising technologies in addition to RFID. We are a lot more excited about the use of these technologies to address counterfeit and stolen drugs versus waiting for RFID to mature. One company has emerged since 2004 that we believe has the technology and business process approach to address these issues. The name of this company is Authentix.

Authentix

Authentix, launched in its present state as a company in 2003, has rapidly become a global leader in authentication solutions for brand protection and fiscal recovery. Authentix is the inventor and developer of many of the leading nano-scale authentication solutions in use today to solve counterfeit, adulteration, and smuggling issues. In the past five years, Authentix has helped its customers recover over $5 billion in lost revenues in the petroleum, pharmaceutical, and consumer goods industries.[21]

We are impressed with the approach Authentix uses to address product authentication in the drug supply chain. This approach involves five major steps, with the objectives of providing revenue recovery and product and brand protection for its customers.[22]

1. **Consulting:** Authentix has subject matter and legislative expertise in the drug supply chain on its pharma industry team. Using this expertise, Authentix is able to assess the impact of counterfeit and stolen drugs on suppliers, distributors, retailers, and patients. In addition, through field sampling and collaboration with government experts (e.g., FDA) and industry executives,

Why Authentix Solutions Are So Secure

In building an authentication solution, Authentix adopts a secure, multi-layered approach that incorporates avert features (visible to the consumer), covert features (restricted to authorized inspectors), and a combination of forensic features (the pecence and identity of which is closely guarded) to ensure product surety.

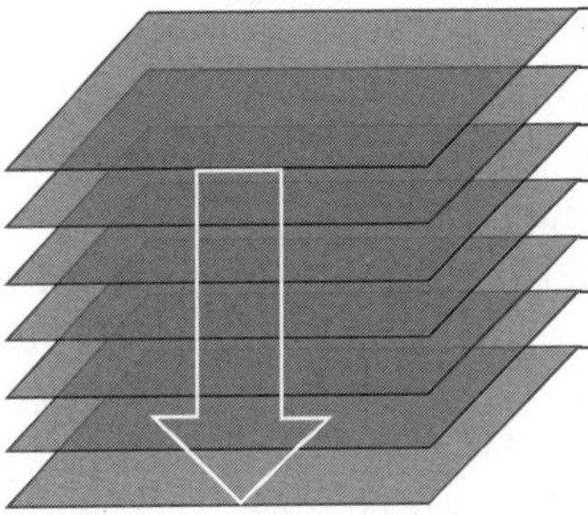

Depth of Security		Example Technologies	
	Overt	Color Shifting Ink	Field Visual
	Covert	Pen Revealable Marker	Field Disposable
	Covert	Pothonic Authentication	Field Instrument
	Covert	Spectral Fingerprint A	Field Instrument
	Forensic	Spectral Fingerprint B	Lab Analysis
	Forensic	Nano-Scale Markers	Lab Analysis
	Track and Trace	Item-Level Serialization	2-D scans at Change of Custody Points

Figure 7.1   The Authentix multilayered authentication solution. Souce: Authentix.

it is able to identify trends and develop forecasts that quantify the negative impact of counterfeit and stolen drugs for its clients.

2. **Mark and authenticate:** If there is a "secret sauce" with Authentix, it is its ability to develop and use overt, covert, and forensic markers. It combines these proprietary markers with a multilayered technology platform (Figure 7.1), including some FDA-accepted markers for in-product marking, that provides clients with package and product authentication through client-specific "marker fingerprints." Authentix develops Web-enabled field authentication devices that read the authentication fingerprints, verify their authenticity, and report any discrepancies. The multilayered approach and covert nature of some of the markers make it very difficult for counterfeiters to devise methods to beat the protection.

3. **Programs:** The Authentix approach to program management includes comprehensive supply chain surveillance. Its supply chain surveillance program starts with unique serialized codes applied to each item during the manufacturing of the drug, with these codes uploaded to a central server. These "covert codes" are linked to any "overt codes" and nested to case and pallet codes. As pallets are sent to a warehouse, pallet codes are matched to the codes on cases and individual units, providing "parent to child" relationships. This step includes the matching of any printed or RFID codes. All codes are associated with customers and specific customer destinations upon shipping dispatch from the warehouse. The pallets and product cases are scanned upon receipt by the distributor. Discrepancies are noted and alerts immediately issued. The pallet and product case codes are matched to retailer or customer

data upon shipping dispatch, with discrepancies reported. The retailer scans all codes upon receipt from the distributor and the placement of the product on the pharmacists' shelves. In addition, their global field monitoring programs help prevent reverse supply chain discrepancies.

4. **Information and integration services:** The supply chain surveillance programs rely on proprietary middleware that can interface with all operating platforms. Authentix uses the discrepancy reporting to provide its clients, and its clients' supply chain partners, with near real-time reporting and event alerts. In addition, clients can secure data-mining services from the Authentix database to track and trace incidents from the point of discrepancy back to the point of intrusion or theft in the drug supply chain.

5. **Investigative compliance enforcement:** Recognizing the importance of compliance to federal, state, and local laws, Authentix developed the capability to support compliance enforcement. It uses its capabilities to create case files, provide investigative services, provide accurate chain of evidence custody records, and provide "expert witness" litigation support to its clients harmed by counterfeit or stolen drugs.

We are very impressed by the approach, the technology, and the successful case studies of Authentix. What we do not understand is why the FDA Counterfeit Drug Task Force continues to endorse RFID as their technology of the future (and up to 10 years is not the near future) when alternative track-and-trace *and* authentication technologies are available as you read this book. In addition, the task force clearly identified alternative technologies as "promising" in its 2004 report. The authors are not investors in Authentix (we may be in the future!), but we are impressed that solutions are available today to address counterfeit and stolen drugs in the drug supply chain.

In addition, we mentioned before that the "bad guys" have made progress since 2004. It takes a high level of "smarts" (and money) to duplicate drug manufacturing facilities, packaging, and labels. If they can chemically decompose the formulas for sophisticated drugs, the "bad guys" can most certainly duplicate RFID tags and introduce counterfeit RFID tag readers that steal or pass along "fake" RFID signals. This unfortunate fact is why we believe the Authentix technique of using covert markers is so compelling.

Summary and Our Recommendations

Despite the best efforts of the FDA and a few key drug supply chain participants, the issue of counterfeit and stolen drugs in the drug supply chain has increased significantly during the past several years. Not only are lost profits and brand degradation at risk, but literally the lives of patients relying on these drugs for their medical care.

We recommend the following for the FDA and the drug industry supply chain:

1. Using a small but elite group of industry, technology, and government "experts," develop a pro forma set of standards to govern common product data flow.
2. Together with the top executives of the pharmaceutical, healthcare, and distribution companies, aggressively lobby Congress to adopt these standards as national standards.
3. If needed, adjust and internationalize the elite group to work with WHO, Interpol, and other international agencies to modify or adopt international standards for common product data flow.
4. Continue to pursue RFID technology for e-pedigree, but shift emphasis on this technology from "a leading technology" to "a complementary technology" in addressing counterfeit and stolen drugs.
5. Aggressively pursue alternative technologies such as color-shifting inks, holograms, and chemical markers incorporated into a drug or label. Perhaps have Authentix or an Authentix-like company work with the senior executives of the top pharmaceutical, healthcare, and distribution companies (and the FDA) to map out the use and standardization of nano-technologies throughout the drug supply chain. Compare and contrast the timing and the value proposition of the alternative technologies versus RFID.
6. Take an aggressive, vigilant role in alternative supply chains such as reverse logistics and Internet sales to eliminate areas of opportunity for the "bad guys."

Notes

1. http://www.nationmaster.com/red/graph/hea_lif_exp_at_bir_tot_pop-lif-expectancy-birth-total-population.
2. http://en.wikipedia.org/wiki/Population_ageing.
3. Discussion with VP of Supply Chain, major U.S.-based Pharmaceutical company, June 2007, Indianapolis, Indiana.
4. http://en.wikipedia.org/wiki/Counterfeit_drug.
5. Martinez, Barbara and Goldstein, Jacob. "Big Pharma Faces Grim Prognosis." *The Wall Street Journal*, December 6, 2007, A1 and A14.
6. Ibid.
7. http://www.who.int/mediacentre/factsheets/fs275/en/print.html, World Health Organization, Fact Sheet #275, November 14, 2006.
8. Ibid.
9. http://www.fda.gov/fdac/features/2004/304_drug.html, U.S. Food and Drug Administration, "Protecting Consumers from Counterfeit Drugs," May–June Issue, 2004.
10. Ibid.
11. http://www.fda.gov/cder/regulatory/PDMA/default.htm.

12. http://www.fda/gov/oc/initiatives/counterfeit/cpg.html, DRAFT COMPLIANCE POL-ICY GUIDE 160.900, "Prescription Drug Marketing Act—Pedigree Requirements under 21 CFR Part 203, June 2006.

13. http://www.who.int/mediacentre/factsheets/fs275/en/print.html, "Counterfeiting grows more sophisticated," World Health Organization, Fact Sheet #275, November 14, 2006.

14. Ibid.

15. http://www.nytimes.com/2007/05/06/world/americas/06poison.html?_r=1&oref=slogin, "From China to Panama, a Trail of Poisoned Medicine," by Walt Bogdanich and Jake Hooker, May 6, 2007.

16. http://www.retailsolutions.com/pdfs/Prod.Authentication.v1.jan.17.07.pdf.

17. http://www.usdoj.gov/ndic/pubs21/21137/index.htm, National Drug Threat Assessment 2007, USDA, October, 2006.

18. http://www.sciencedaily.com/releases/2008/07/080717221157.htm, Risks in Ordering Drugs By Internet On The Rise, July 20, 2008.

19. Ibid.

20. Tour of CLS MedTurn Fort Worth facility with Harold Anderson, area director.

21. Authentix Overview Presentation, July 2008.

22. Ibid.

Chapter 8

The Near Future for Technology in Supply Chain Management

Technology, like art, is a soaring exercise of the human imagination....
Technology is the instrumental ordering of human experience within
a logic of efficient means, and the direction of nature to use its powers
for material gain.

Daniel Bell, "Technology, Nature, and Society"

Technology...the knack of so arranging the world that we don't have
to experience it.

Max Frisch, "Second Stop"

Introduction

Over the past 15 or so years, enterprise solution providers (software companies,
systems integrators, and consultants) have very successfully persuaded companies
to replace their proprietary systems with "off-the-shelf" solutions. These solutions
have now become the transactional backbones for these companies, and, accord-
ingly, are very difficult to replace. However, whether deployed in finance, human
resources, sales, or the supply chain, these solutions are primarily focused on solving

the problems within the enterprise or silos within the enterprise. For the most part, solving cross-functional or inter-enterprise problems remains beyond their capabilities. In addition, these solutions have predetermined workflows that "pour in concrete" a company's method for handling business processes.

In researching this book, the authors reviewed a number of requests for proposals (RFPs) issued by major high-tech manufacturers. These companies were asking for help solving what has become a very common problem: managing the extended supply chain when manufacturing is outsourced to Asia-based (primarily Chinese) companies. What was illuminating about these RFPs was not the specifics of the process, which are very familiar to the authors (who have years of experience in international logistics), but rather the admission in the documents that neither the physical nor informational portions of the problem could be solved by a single provider.

We believe that solving cross-functional and inter-enterprise information system challenges still represents a major enterprise software opportunity. The extended supply chain domain represents only part of the opportunity but is a major portion of the overall problem.

Cross-Functional Supply Chain Problems and Inter-Enterprise Collaboration Problems

Supply chain costs represent approximately 10% of the gross domestic product of the United States and other advanced economies. For the United States in 2003–2006, this represents more than $1 trillion in annual expenditures of which about 60% is transportation related, 30% is inventory-carrying costs (warehousing, interest, obsolescence, etc.), with the balance spent on administration and information technology costs.[1]

Moving products through the supply chain involves an intricate dance between original equipment manufacturers (OEMs), transportation asset providers, service providers, and the enterprise's internal functions. Choreographing this dance requires a tremendous amount of information to flow between the parties. Value-added networks (VANs) such as Sterling Commerce, Kleinschmidt, and others sprang up to provide connectivity between the companies' transactional systems, but increasingly this service is performed using the Internet. Electronic Data Interchange (EDI) standards were developed to allow companies to exchange data in a common format using VANs (Figure 8.1). As of the date of this book, EDI formats continue to carry the majority of the information payload between companies, but XML (extensible markup language) formats are increasingly popular.

This collaboration between players in the supply chain can be boiled down to a simple "signaling" process: customers send a demand signal (via a retailer or distributor) to the manufacturer, who in turn signals its OEMs and service providers to make, transport, and deliver the desired product(s).

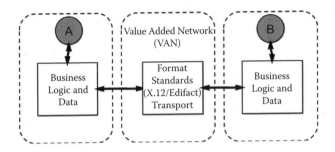

Figure 8.1   The value-added network exchange model.

Companies that execute this signaling process best enjoy lower costs and higher margins than their competitors because their order to cash cycle is shortened (Dell Computer and Wal-Mart, for example). In general, VAN-based EDI does a good job of handling the process when the players are sophisticated, operate at high volume, and the products are simple. However, as manufacturing is "off-shored," less experienced companies are introduced into the chain, transport links are made longer, and products increase in complexity while life cycles are shortened, the traditional VAN-based processes become less than optimal.

Stage Is Set for Inter-Enterprise Process Fusion

Beginning in the mid-1990s, technology companies and consulting firms encouraged companies to rip out their proprietary systems and install "off-the-shelf solutions" from enterprise software vendors. Much of this work was driven by Y2K related fears and the technology bubble.

Despite all the horror stories of failed implementations and budget overruns, the reality is that many companies, if not most, did derive benefits from the implementation of new systems as their internal, transaction backbones systems. A backbone system is defined as a transmission network that carries high-speed telecommunications between regions (e.g., a nationwide long-distance telephone system). It is sometimes used to describe the part of a local area network that carries signals between branching points. This contention is supported, in macroeconomic terms, by rapidly rising productivity, especially in the United States.

However, the benefits of these new enterprise systems rarely extended outside the companies to their business partners. In addition, the authors would contend that many of the economic benefits gained over the past 10 years are "one time" in nature, resulting from better utilization of labor, especially with offshore suppliers, and increased capital investment, especially in computer systems. However, as any economics student knows, labor and capital increases cannot continue forever in the face of diminishing returns. Instead, technology or "know how" is the secret ingredient that enables continuously rising productivity and, as a result, economic growth. It is no longer enough to switch to a supplier in a low-wage country and

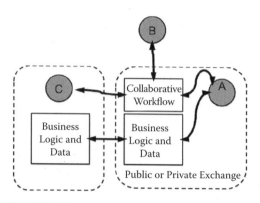

Figure 8.2   The extended enterprise model.

throw computers at white-collar workers. Instead, leading companies must learn how to share knowledge and improve business processes with their trading partners, regardless of where they are located.

The 1980s and 1990s belonged to technology companies that spurred personal and intra-enterprise productivity. This decade and the next will belong to the technology companies that increase inter-enterprise productivity.

Extended Enterprise: Right Idea, Wrong Architecture

Along with the Internet bubble, the concept of trading exchanges was introduced as the solution to inter-enterprise collaboration. Most of these evolved as an "extended enterprise" model as illustrated in Figure 8.2. In this model, all participants (companies A, B, and C in the diagram) share a common data repository that prescribes a collaborative workflow.

Unfortunately, the extended enterprise model ignores the differences between trading partners. Only highly standardized collaborative processes can be supported within this framework. In addition, because the model involves taking a single instance of an enterprise solution deployed for one participant (SAP's enterprise resource planning, for example) and extending it to autonomous organizations, a host of issues regarding data ownership, security, and process flexibility are created.

Rise of Web Services

At the other end of the spectrum from the tightly controlled, inflexible extended enterprise is the world of "Web services." Web services are defined as "a software system designed to support interoperable Machine to Machine interaction over a network."[3] Web services are Web-based applications that use XML standards and transport protocols to exchange data with client software programs. What's nice about Web services is that a company can define whatever functions it wants and then expose these functions to their business partners in the supply chain. It could be as simple as a function that accepts a tracking number and returns a location or something as complicated as a set of functions for creating and managing entire orders.

Over the past few years consumer and small enterprise oriented Web sites have really taken up Web services and are leading the way in showing the types of interesting applications that can be created by simply giving your customers access to Web services. Examples include Google Maps, the Facebook Developer platform, and Salesforce.com's Apex.

Through Web services, programmers can access the services of a variety of partners and combine these services into composite applications sometimes called "mash-ups." These composite applications can be developed quickly and cheaply and are infinitely flexible. Most of the major business software application providers "eat their own dog food" and build their new application Web services so that the same methods used to access the application engine features can be made available to outside parties (at least in part).

Web services are part of the evolution to Service Oriented Architecture (SOA) as the dominant model for large-scale application development today. SOA is an outgrowth of traditional ideas of distributed computing and modular programming. SOAs build applications out of services with relatively large units of functionality that humans readily recognize as service such as "placing an order" or "booking an airline ticket." The goal of an SOA is to be able to build ad hoc applications entirely (or almost entirely) from existing services—the composite applications or mash-ups mentioned above.

From a supply chain point of view, Web services are clearly appealing. Supply chains constantly evolve with new players coming into the network of relationships and other ones dropping out. The question for supply chain professionals is, how to bring order to a constantly evolving supply chain? Can Web services really address the continuum from casual users creating a mash-up to track their order via Google Maps to a critical supplier who makes key components on a top selling product?

Federated Enterprise Concept

In parallel to the advent of Web services, the International Organization for Standardization, along with commercial and governmental participants, has been developing standards for how these technologies can be used in a structured fashion to help trading partners perform electronic business in a secure, reproducible way according to agreed upon business processes.[4] For simplicity's sake, we'll call this the "federated enterprise" concept. In a federated enterprise, the process of collaboration is based on a combination of joint (externally based) and internal criteria, but each participant maintains its own internal workflow, business procedures, and routines. The federated enterprise architecture does not prescribe or require that a set of processes be followed or a set of data be exchanged in order to proceed with collaboration. Instead, the architecture creates a framework for managing shared objectives across organizations. Data is not simply replicated, it is shared in the specific context required for the collaborative event to proceed.

This type of collaborative model enables partners to work together on common business objectives, while providing flexibility internally to pursue autonomous strategies and independent processes. This federated enterprise model also allows participants to have varying levels of process integration. Casual users can access publicly available Web services while close partners may get access to much more detailed and confidential data.

Deploying the Federated Enterprise Architecture[4]

Unlike the extended enterprise solution, which entails strong-arming partners into participation, developing rigid workflows, and high costs, the federated enterprise model (Figure 8.3) promises a three-step process that breaks down the barriers to adoption:

1. Enabling the system: Participants deploy an open standard gateway based on Web services or another XML-based standards to expose internal data to a structured interface.
2. Allowing connectivity: Participants allow connections to federation servers that host open schema models, enabling publishing and subscribing to the data in those schemas. For example, in a supply chain application, a set of entities such as the advanced shipping notice, purchase order, or schedule agreement would be made available on the federation server. Obviously, participants can control the level of access they wish to grant trading partners.
3. Adopting collaborative workflow: Participants need to understand their own internal processes before adopting value-added collaboration. They need to know the location, quality, and security considerations of the data to be shared.

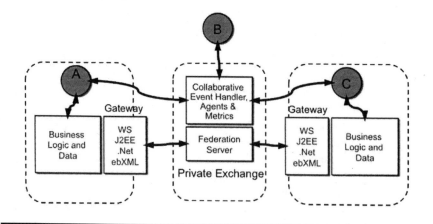

Figure 8.3   The federated enterprise model.

With these pieces in place they can then describe to partners the requirements for collaboration in a standard fashion in a public or semi-public repository.

Why Are Web Services Better Than What Came Before?

Any veteran of the technology industry is typically pretty jaded when they hear about the "next big thing" that will allow collaboration, especially when it involves the complexities of the supply chain. So why is the SOA concept different? In short, the concept seems to strike a balance between the requirements for standards and the need to be flexible that matches up with how enterprises act in the real world. Companies are not forced to buy a particular software package. They can buy or develop their Web services in Java or .Net Framework, or they can create "wrappers" around legacy applications that make them act like Web services. A company can decide to open up all, none, or some of its business processes to customers and trading partners based on the specifics of their industry and competitive situation. Finally, Web services are easy to get started with. A company can "get its feet wet" quickly and easily with some simple applications and ride up the complexity curve at a pace that suits its business.

Private Initiatives in Creating Inter-Enterprise Systems: Multiparty Networks

While many of the ideas in the federated architecture are well accepted, getting entire industries to adopt standards and coordinate their internal information technology development toward a common goal is often impossible. At the end of the 1990s, a lot of effort went into developing the concept of "industry exchanges," where large participants in vertical markets, such as auto, semiconducters, and food, got together in joint ventures to "own" the value chain process management in that vertical market. For the most part, these efforts failed miserably. However, a number of these networks have survived and prospered and point the way to true enterprise scale multiparty systems that can revolutionize not only the supply chain but other business with similar features as well.

Two good examples of successful industry networks are OneNetwork (www.onenetwork.com) in retail and defense and iTrade (www.itradenetwork.com) in grocery and produce. In OneNetwork's case, they've built a network processing backbone that lets participants define their own processes and optimizations. Participants can then invite their trading partners to join. Unlike an ERP system, OneNetwork provides "one version of the truth" because the data is stored on the network. Participant "perspectives" allow the various parties to determine what data they will and won't share, and a "tunable system of control" allows each party to set the system of record in their process (their ERP versus OneNetwork, for example). The result is a very flexible, fast-deploying system for managing complex supply chain processes. The network also features a studio (for business analysts) and a software development kit for programmers so that participants can quickly design new applications.

Big Three: Identification, Location, and Condition

It's easy to boil down supply chain information requirements to three essential elements:

1. *What is it?* It is a unique identification of the product or asset. Unfortunately, in today's world of counterfeit products, part of identification must also be "authentication"—is it real?
2. *Where is it?* It involves locating it with a sufficient degree of accuracy to be useful.
3. *How is it?* What is its condition? Did it get too hot or cold? Is it broken?

If enterprises where able to get this information in real time or near real time from their inventory and assets, they could make significant strides in productivity and profitability (Figure 8.4).

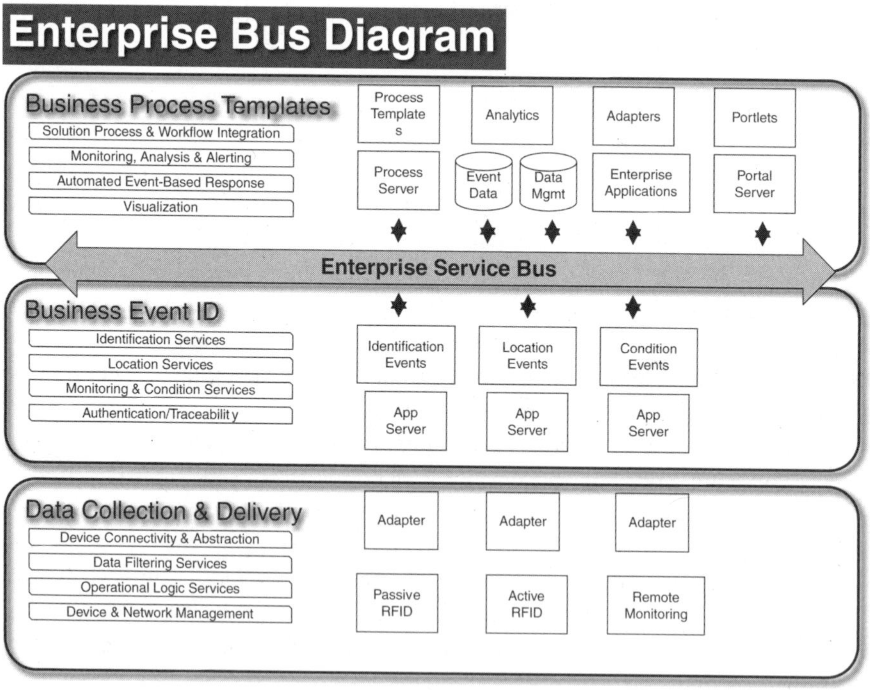

Figure 8.4 The enterprise business diagram.

A look at large-scale experiments in the supply chain by major players like the U.S. Department of Defense and Wal-Mart involving passive and active RFID and remote monitoring shows that all are efforts to get this "what, where, and how" information back to the systems and people so that better decisions can be made.

Information Security—The Key to Enabling Data Flow

An underlying assumption throughout this book is that data moving to and from devices and enterprises is "secure." This is a big assumption, given the convergence of technologies that enable mobile devices, voice over Internet phones, and multimedia devices to move data to an enterprise.

The challenge comes when a mobile worker, remote worker, or remote device is using the Internet (Web services) to send data to and retrieve information from the enterprise. Once the enterprise firewall recognizes the device and allows it access to the enterprise, all enterprise information is at risk. Hackers are smart and can penetrate enterprise firewalls in numerous ways.

Hackers can place a rogue phone device within the company. This is sometimes difficult to do without inside access. Rogue employees of the enterprise or the telephone repair service could do the trick. Hackers can also infect a desktop or personal computer within the enterprise. Through the rogue remote device, a hacker can "take over" the desktop or personal computer and download any and all accessible information in the enterprise. These actions can take place without the operator of the desktop or the personal computer being aware of what is happening with their computer equipment.

Steps must be taken by chief information officers to secure their data. The Internet protocol private branch exchanges and phones must be tested for rogue devices and irregularities. This can be done through the authentication of all data-sharing devices and all users. Strong policies are needed, backed by robust enforcement to discourage any and all illegal activities. In addition, firewalls, communications protocols, and security measures need to be tested on an on-going basis.

The exposure is significant. Let us go back to the devices on ocean containers for supply chain participants to remotely monitor temperature, humidity, gases, and location. These devices will undoubtedly have maintenance issues throughout their life cycles. The mere fact that a repair center can "swap out" problem devices with new devices represents a process-based vulnerability. Rogue employees or hackers can introduce a rogue device for a good device during the maintenance process. Unless there are layered authentication tests on the new device, the enterprise may be vulnerable to the introduction of a rogue device.

There are other points of vulnerability as well. The OEM assembler of the device, the contract developers interfacing the device to the sensors, the communications workers helping the carriers recognize and approve the devices on their networks,

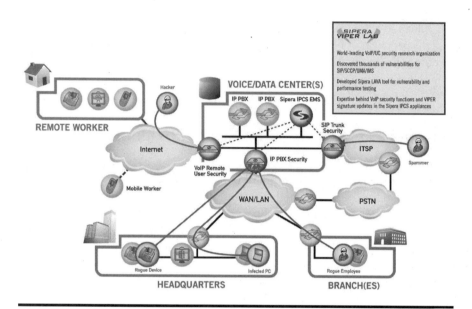

Figure 8.5   Sipera Systems' Viper Lab.

and the hosted "back-end" systems providers linking the data to enterprise systems all represent vulnerability points for rogue employees or hackers.

One company is working hard to provide information security layers to enterprises. Sipera Systems of Richardson, Texas, has developed its "Sipera Viper Lab" to test an enterprise's vulnerability to a rogue attack. Using its "Sipera LAVA" tool and a group of the best hackers in the marketplace, Sipera can test the enterprise's vulnerability to rogue attacks over the Internet, through wireless and local area networks, inside the enterprise, and outside the enterprise (authenticated device to another device). Vulnerabilities are identified and published to the stakeholders responsible within the enterprise for risk management (Figure 8.5).

The professional hackers are downright scary. The authors have watched these men and women invade the "privacy" of the enterprise and its device users and access any or all data they want. Corporate sales, marketing, manufacturing, financial, and supply chain data are all at risk. In addition, individual employees are at risk as well. In today's world of online banking, Internet purchases, and personal interactions through instant messaging and emails, these hackers can steal the identity of an individual in lightning-quick fashion.

Chief information officers and chief financial officers must recognize the future of Web services, the benefits of openly sharing data throughout the global supply chain, and the risks associated with the sharing of data. In our opinion, the wrong action to take is to retrench and not share the appropriate data with supply chain partners. Another wrong action is to do nothing and assume all is well, as devices sharing data proliferate in number throughout the enterprise and its supply chains.

The correct action is to review the vulnerabilities of the enterprise and take the necessary action to secure data-sharing to and from the enterprise.

Enterprise Framework for the Future

Consensus is emerging in the business community about the future of enterprise systems:

1. They are being built using the Service Oriented Architecture concept.
2. They are utilizing real-time or near real-time data collection and delivery via passive and active RFID, wireless communications, and new types of sensors.
3. They use Web services to link both within the organization and to outside parties.
4. They assume heterogeneous systems and networks.
5. They are designed to be loosely coupled so that change and enhancement are embraced rather than feared.
6. They are aggressive in protecting the information security of the enterprise.
7. They are built assuming a large variety of roles and levels of trust for the users of the system.

Notes

1. Global Sourcing Presentation, Kuglin, Inc., January 2007.
2. http://www.timbercon.com/Backbone-System.html, "Backbone System."
3. http://en.wikipedia.com/wiki/Web_services, and Web Services Glossary.
4. ISO/TS 15000-2:2004. http://www.iso.org/iso/en/CatalogueDetailPage.CatalogueDetail? CSNUMBER=39972.
5. http://www.ebxmlsoft.com/papers/ebxmi-fera.pdf, "ebXML and Federated Enterprise Reference Architecture (EFERA)," Goran Zugic, Chief Architect, ebXMLsoft Inc., July 21, 2003.

Index